THE BASIS AND
ESSENTIALS OF
FRENCH

———◆———

THE BASIS AND ESSENTIALS OF
FRENCH

———◆———

Containing all that must be known of
Grammar, Vocabulary and Idioms for
most everyday purposes by
CHARLES DUFF
Revised and partly rewritten by
Madeleine James, F.I.L.

NELSON

THOMAS NELSON AND SONS LTD
36 Park Street London W1
P.O. Box 336 Apapa Lagos
P.O. Box 25012 Nairobi
P.O. Box 21149 Dar es Salaam
P.O. Box 2187 Accra
77 Coffee Street San Fernando Trinidad

THOMAS NELSON (AUSTRALIA) LTD
597 Little Collins Street Melbourne C1

THOMAS NELSON AND SONS (SOUTH AFRICA) (PROPRIETARY) LTD
51 Commissioner Street Johannesburg

THOMAS NELSON AND SONS (CANADA) LTD
81 Curlew Drive Don Mills Ontario

THOMAS NELSON AND SONS
Copewood and Davis Streets Camden New Jersey 08103

First published 1935
This extensively revised edition published 1969

17 146062 6

Printed in Great Britain by
William Clowes and Sons, Limited, London and Beccles
for Thomas Nelson and Sons Ltd, 36 Park Street, London W1

CONTENTS

————◆————

Contents

PART 2
THE ESSENTIAL VOCABULARY

Vocabulary 79

Essential vocabulary 82

ABBREVIATIONS

abbr	abbreviation	pl	plural
adj	adjective	pop	popular speech
adv	adverb	poss	possessive
aux	auxiliary	pr	pronounce, pronunciation
coll	colloquial		
conj	conjunction	prep	preposition
def	definite	pres	present
dem	demonstrative	pron	pronoun
disj	disjunctive	qch	quelque chose, something
f, fem	feminine	qn	quelqu'un, somebody
fam	familiar	rel	relative
fut	future	s, sing	singular
imp	imperfect	sb	somebody
imper	imperative	sth	something
impers	impersonal	subj	subjunctive
ind	indicative	tr	transitive
indef	indefinite	v	verb
inf	infinitive	vaux	auxiliary verb
inter	interrogative	vintr	intransitive verb
intr	intransitive	vtr	transitive verb
inv	invariable		
irr	irregular		
m, masc	masculine		
n	noun		
num	numeral		
OC	orthographic change(s)		
pa	past		
part	participle		
pers	person, personal		

Classification of verbs:

  I indicates a Group I verb (pp. 46–7.)

  II indicates a Group II verb (p. 47.)

III indicates a Group III verb (pp. 47–8.)

  See also p. 45.

PART 1

THE BASIS OF GRAMMAR

◆

ALPHABET AND PRONUNCIATION

French uses the same twenty-six letters as those of the English alphabet. In addition, French uses 'accents' or, more correctly, diacritical signs:

Accents: (´) called the acute accent, written over the vowel **e** as in **une étude** *a study*, and **la journée** *the day*.

(`) the grave accent, used mainly over the letter *e* as in **le père** *the father*, **la mère** *the mother*. In some instances it is used to differentiate the meanings of words that would otherwise be written similarly. Thus: **ou** *or*; **où** *where*. **a** *has*; **à** *to, at* (prep).

(^) the circumflex accent, may be used over any vowel and usually affects the sound: **l'âge** *age*, **être** *to be*, **une île** *an island*, **un impôt** *a tax*, **mûr** *ripe, mature*.

The cedilla (¸), used under the letter **c** (pronounced -ss- before **e, i**) to indicate when the hissing sound must be retained before the hard vowels **a, o, u**. Thus: **ça** *that*, **français** *French*, **reçu** *received*.

The diaeresis (¨) is used when two vowels come together to indicate that the vowel over which it is written must be pronounced separately from the vowel which precedes. Thus: **Noël** *Christmas*.

Standard French pronunciation: The foreigner should aim to achieve a pronunciation which is as close as possible to that of the educated Parisian.

Written French and spoken French: As in English, the same sound is sometimes represented by different combinations of letters. In other words, French spelling very often is not a phonetic representation of the spoken language. To take only one example of how confusing this can be for the absolute beginner, consider these words: l'**an**, nag**eant**, **en**, **en**voyer, l'acc**ent**, l'**am**bre, **em**ployer. The parts of these words in heavy type, although spelt

an, eant, en, ent, am, em

represent only one sound, which can be symbolized thus ã. This symbol is taken from the International Phonetic Alphabet (IPA), which provides one symbol for one sound. Symbols for all the sounds of French are given in the pages which follow, each one with words written in normal French to show how that sound is represented in print.

As the French sounds represent speech-habits very different from those of English, they must be heard in order that they may be reproduced accurately. See *Points to note* on p. 10.

PHONETICS: LA PHONÉTIQUE

IPA symbol and key word	French words to exemplify the sound represented by the IPA symbol	Letters used for the sound in written French
	1. Vowel sounds	
i si	(a) il, ici, ville, si (b) y, bicyclette	i y
e et	(a) été, café, passé (b) et (= and) (c) parler (d) parlez (e) parlerai	é et er ez ai
ɛ le lait	(a) après, pièce (b) poulet, ouest, des, quel (c) faible, aimez, français, lait (d) plaît (e) est (= is) (f) hiver, erreur (g) même, fête	ès, è et, e, es, e ai, ais, ait aît est e ê
a la	(a) la, va, ça, gare (b) États-Unis, chocolat (c) à, voilà, déjà (d) moi, voir, fois	a at à oi, ois (pr = wa)
ɑ pâle	(a) pas, cas, bas (b) cassez, tasse (c) pâle (d) crois, mois, froid	as a â ois, oid (pr = wah)

IPA symbol and key word	French words to exemplify the sound represented by the IPA symbol	Letters used for the sound in written French

1. Vowel sounds *(continued)*

ɔ la poste	(a) école, poste, encore (b) restaurant (c) hôpital, rôti	o au ô
o l'eau	(a) au, aux, chaud, auto (b) beau, bateau, bureau, l'eau (c) chose, auto, vos (d) tôt, le vôtre (e) oh!	au, aux, aud, au eau, eaux o ô oh
u ou	(a) fou, tout, jour, ou (b) où (c) ragoût	ou où oû
y la rue	(a) du, perdu, vu, avenue, rue (b) autobus, dure (c) sûr	u, ue u û
φ deux	(a) peu, Dieu, feu (b) deux, ceux, peut (c) Monsieur (d) œufs	eu eux, eut eur œufs
œ bœuf	(a) heure, neuf, seul (b) l'œuf, cœur, bœuf	eu œu
ə je	(a) le, je, ce, que, de, me, ne (b) prenez, venez, menu (c) premier, semaine	e e e

2. Nasal vowels

| ɛ̃

vin | (a) vin, cinq, vingt

(b) main, demain, saint
(c) rien, bien, mien, combien
(d) faim | in, inq, ingt

ain, aint
(i)en
aim   (in, im not followed by a vowel) |

IPA symbol and key word	French words to exemplify the sound represented by the IPA symbol	Letters used for the sound in written French
ɑ̃ blanc	(a) **an, quand, quant, dans** (b) **en, enveloppe, souvent** (c) **jambon, blanc** (d) **emporter**	**an, and,**　(**an, am** **ant, ans**　not **en, ent**　fol- **am, anc**　lowed **em**　　　by a 　　　　　vowel)
ɔ̃ bon	(a) **on, mon, sont, parlons, non** (b) **nom, ombre, combien**	**on, om** not fol- 　lowed by a vowel
œ̃ un	**un, brun, parfum** Mnemonic for the four nasal 　vowels	**un, um** not fol- 　lowed by a vowel **un bon vin blanc**

3. Semi-vowels

j le pied	(a) **pied, bien, avion, monsieur** (b) **voyons, voyage, voyageur** (c) **billet, fille**	**i, y** followed by a 　vowel or liquid 　**-ll**
:j le soleil	**appareil, réveil, réveille** **soleil, travail, essaye**	final **-il, -ille** 　(and **-ye**) pre- 　ceded by a vowel
w le froid	(a) Sound **u** followed by sound **i**: 　　**oui** (b) Sound **u** followed by sound **a**: 　　**soir, toit** (c) Sound **u** followed by sound **ɑ**: 　　**crois, froid** (d) Sound **u** followed by sound **ɛ̃**: 　　**moins**	similar to English **w**-sound + **i, a,** **ɑ, ɛ̃** Commonest written form is **oi**
ɥ la nuit	Sound **y** followed by sound **i**: **nuit** **huit, suis, pluie**. If followed by 　other vowels, consult a diction- 　ary with phonetics	Usually written **ui, uit, uie, uis**

IPA symbol and key word	French words to exemplify the sound represented by the IPA symbol	Letters used for the sound in written French

4. Consonants

p la pipe	(a) initial: **p**i**p**e, **p**as, **p**our (b) final: Euro**p**e (c) clusters: **pl**ace, a**pp**elez, a**b**solument	**p, pp, pe** sometimes **b** in clusters (example a**b**solument)
b le buffet	(a) **b**ureau, **b**ateau, **b**uffet (b) super**b**e (c) **bl**eu, aima**bl**e	**b, be** **bl** in clusters
t le tennis	(a) **t**ennis, **t**able (b) l'es**t**, l'oues**t**, sep**t**, cigare**tt**e (c) mon**t**re, ques**t**ion, par**t**ir	**t-** **-t, -pt, -tt-** **t** in clusters
d dix	(a) **d**u, **d**ix, **d**ent (b) su**d** (c) aéro**d**rome	**d**
k le coup	(a) **qu**el, **qu**and, **c**arte, **c**oup, é**c**ole (b) cin**q**, ave**c** (c) **k**ilo, **k**épi	**qu, c** before **a, o, u** **-q, c** final **k**
g la gare	(a) **g**are, **g**arçon (b) fati**gu**e (c) a**g**réable, an**g**lais	**g** **gue** **g** in clusters
f la France	(a) **f**eu, **f**ois (b) neu**f**, veu**f** (c) **F**rance, **f**rançais, **f**ront, **fl**air	**f**
v voilà	(a) **v**oici, **v**oilà, **v**ous, veu**f** (b) j'arri**v**e, a**v**enue, veu**v**e (c) **v**rai	**v, ve**
s le sac	(a) **s**ac, ti**ss**u, **sc**ience (b) **c**e, piè**c**e, **c**iel, cin**q** (c) françai**s**, garçon, reçu (d) si**x**, soi**x**ante	**s, ss, sc** **c** before **e** and **i** **ç** before **a, o, u** **x** in si**x**, soi**x**ante

IPA symbol and key word	French words to exemplify the sound represented by the IPA symbol	Letters used for the sound in written French
z la zone	(a) zéro, zone, onze (b) rose, rasoir	z, s between vowels
ʃ le chat	(a) chose, chien, chat (b) blanche, La Manche, chercher	ch (similar to English sh)
ʒ jamais	(a) jour, jamais (b) horloge, manger, gilet	j g before e and i
l le lac	(a) lac, l'est, quel, quelle, allez (b) place, agréable, bleu	l, ll l in clusters
m la maison	(a) mais, maison, même, madame (b) sommes, homme, femme	m, mm
n le nez	(a) nous, nord, nuit, une (b) bonne, vienne (c) journal, moderne	n, nn
ɲ la montagne	never occurs initially (a) montagne, Boulogne (b) gagner	gn (similar to sound in English 'onion')
r le rire	(a) rire, rue, roue, après, erreur (b) heure, merci, sur, vers, vert	r, rr -rs, -rt (r before final consonant)

5. Symbols to aid pronunciation

h always silent	hier, horloge There is liaison before h-mute: un_homme, une_heure	written h
*h	h-'aspirate', not pronounced, but has a glottal stop before it: le *haut, la *honte. There is no liaison with *h	written h in normal French, but *h in the vocabulary to this book

IPA symbol and key word	French words to exemplify the sound represented by the IPA symbol	Letters used for the sound in written French

5. Symbols to aid pronunciation *(Continued)*

| ⌣ les‿amis | in some textbooks, marks words to be joined in liaison: **les‿amis** | not marked in normal French |
| ′ stress mark | not written in normal French but used in the IPA to show that the syllable following is stressed: **le cinéma** (sine′ma) *cinema* | |

Points to note

Many sounds in spoken French are foreign to English-speakers' ears. This is not to say that an English speaker cannot learn to pronounce them, or that he or she cannot acquire a good accent in French. But it would be misleading to say that this can be done easily. It is a matter of listening carefully to a good native speaker, mimicking the sounds heard, and having them corrected when they are badly spoken.

A good French pronunciation cannot be learnt from a book, and attempts at 'imitated' pronunciation in print may do more harm to the learner than good. The learner has to be able to (*a*) recognize the sounds when they are spoken, and (*b*) articulate them accurately, which means clearly. If he cannot do (*a*), he will not understand. If he cannot do (*b*), he will not be understood by a French listener. A bad pronunciation is painful for both speaker and listener.

The best advice that can be given here to the absolute beginner is that he must get a good speaker of French to go through all the sounds listed above, concentrating the greatest effort on the vowels and nasals. The English-speaking beginner usually finds that French **u** and the nasalized vowels are the most difficult sounds to articulate. French **u** = German **ü**. It can be made by shaping the lips to make our oo-sound in moor and saying ee (i) at the same time. Listen and mimic must be the rule, as well as frequent practice and repetition, until all the sounds are mastered. The words given to illustrate the sounds should be pronounced (their meanings can be learnt later).

Once the sounds are known, the beginner can start listening to

French radio broadcasts or gramophone records. At first all he need do is to try to catch sounds and reproduce them. It requires consistent and unremitting practice for some time in order to become a fluent speaker. Never miss an opportunity of speaking French with French people.

STRESS IN FRENCH

In English, every word of more than one syllable usually has a syllable that is more strongly stressed than the others. Thus, ab*a*ndon, abr*u*pt, imm*a*culate—the vowels in italic show the stressed syllables.

Stress in French is in contrast to this, and is never very marked. It invariably falls on the last syllable of a group of syllables. Thus **Où allez-vous aujourd'hui?** In this sentence all syllables are equally stressed except the last in **aujourd'hui**. In an isolated word, the last syllable is stressed. Thus: **Comment?**—only -ment is stressed.

LIAISON: 'LINKING'

The words in a spoken sentence in French are always closely knit together within groups or clauses. Within these they run into one another, each word being, as it were, connected with the one before and the one after. There is throughout the spoken language a consistent tendency to carry over the last pronounced consonant of one word on to the syllable which follows it. Thus: **Aujourd'hui je pars à Paris**—this is pronounced as though it were one long word: **Oʒur-dɥiʒəpaːr-a-Pa′ri**, with stress on the final syllable.

In order to make this speech-system easier in practice, the French introduce liaison or the linking together of certain words within a group. This occurs when a word ends with a mute consonant and the next word begins with a vowel or *h*-mute. Thus **les amis** is pronounced as though it were written **lezami**, and **pas encore** is pronounced as **pazã′kɔːr**. This 'linking' is marked in textbooks thus: **les‿amis, pas‿encore**—the liaison sign (‿) is never shown in normal written French, nor is the stress sign (′).

The important factor in 'linking' is that it can only occur within a group of words that are grammatically connected with one another.

Liaison is best learnt by experience in listening to French spoken by good speakers. Note the following points:

s, x and z when linked to the next word are pronounced like z.
t final is usually linked to a vowel following, but not in the word **et** *and*.
r is the infinitive verb ending **-er** does not link.
p is linked only in the words **trop, beaucoup**.
d when linked takes a t-sound: **un grand homme, répond-il?**
final **n** of an adjective followed by a noun beginning with a vowel is denasalized in liaison. Thus: **l'ancien_ami**.

Liaison is often, finally, a matter of taste. Use sparingly until the language is fairly well known.

ELISION

Elision is the suppression of a vowel in the interest of euphony. An apostrophe replaces the removed vowel in written French. Thus

      de, je, jusque, la, le, me, ne, que, se, te
become **d', j', jusqu', l', l', m', n', qu', s', t'**
before a vowel or *h*-mute:
e.g. **j'ai, l'arbre, l'histoire**

GRAVE ACCENT ON CERTAIN WORDS

The grave accent (`) is used on certain words to mark a distinction in grammatical categories but does not alter the sound of the vowel. These must be known:

a *has*	**à** *to*
la *the*	**là** *there*
ou *or*	**où** *where*
des *of the*	**dès** *since, from*
ça *that*	**çà** *hither*

CAPITAL LETTERS AND SMALL LETTERS

Capital letters are not used in French for days of the week, months of the year, seasons, and adjectives of nationality, or in personal titles. But they are used for proper nouns. Thus, when an adjective of nationality is used as a noun, it has a capital letter:

> **Mon ami est de nationalité anglaise** *My friend is English by nationality*

But: **Mon ami est Anglais** *My friend is an Englishman*
> **Elle est Anglaise** *She is an Englishwoman*

Note: Capital letters are not used as much as they are in English.

> **l'évêque de Londres** *the Bishop of London*
> **le prince de Galles** *the Prince of Wales*

ARMES ARTICLES

In English *a*, *an* are indefinite articles; *the* is the definite article. The use of the corresponding articles in French differs from that of our English articles. For example, as every noun in French is either masculine (m) or feminine (f) in gender, there is an article form for each gender, and a plural form. Articles agree in gender and number with their noun.

INDEFINITE ARTICLE

	m	f		
Singular:	**un** *a, an*	**une** *a, an*	**un homme** *a man*	**une femme** *a woman*
Plural:	**des** *some*	**des** *some*	**des hommes** *(some) men*	**des femmes** *(some) women*

The indefinite article is omitted before a noun of status, profession, occupation, rank or nationality:

> **Il est veuf** *He is a widower*
> **Il est médecin** *He is a doctor*
> **Cet homme est boulanger** *This man is a baker*
> **Elle est Italienne** *She is an Italian (woman)*

Des becomes **de** when the qualifying adjective comes before the noun, or after a negative:

> **Ce sont des livres** *They are books*
> **Ce sont de beaux livres** *They are fine (beautiful) books*
> **Il n'y a pas de livres** *There are no books*

DEFINITE ARTICLE

	m	f
Sing:	**Le père** *the father*	**la mère** *the mother*
Pl (both genders):	**Les pères**	**les mères**

L'homme (m), **l'école** (f)—**l'** before a vowel or **h**-mute, both genders.

Contractions

de le is contracted to **du** before a m noun, except when starting with a vowel, or h-mute, when it becomes **de l'**:

> **le mouchoir du garçon** *the boy's handkerchief*
> **les feuilles de l'arbre** *the leaves of the tree*

à le is contracted to **au** before a m noun, except when starting with a vowel or h-mute, when it becomes **à l'**:

> **je parle au garçon** *I speak to the boy*
> **je parle à l'homme** *I speak to the man*

sing m	sing f	plural	
du, de l' *of the*	**de la, de l'**	**des**	} both genders
au, à l' *at the, to the*	**à la, à l'**	**aux**	

PARTITIVE ARTICLE

The partitive article **du, de la, des, de l'** (f and m when noun begins with vowel or h-mute) expresses 'some', 'a little of', 'a piece of', etc.
Je veux manger du pain et boire du café *I want to eat some bread and drink some coffee*

Note: **du pain, de l'eau et des pommes de terre**

Preposition **de** replaces **du, de la, des**:

1. after negative: **Je ne veux pas de pain, de café**

> *I do not want any bread, coffee*

2. after **beaucoup** *much, many, a lot*:

> **J'ai beaucoup de livres** *I have many books*
> **Il a beaucoup d'argent** *he has a lot of money*

Similarly after **une foule de** *a crowd of*, **peu de** *little (of)*, **plein de** *full of*, **trop de** *too much of*.
But **bien de** *much, many (of)* takes the article: **bien du mal** *much evil, badness*, **bien des choses** *many things*.

OTHER USES OF THE DEFINITE ARTICLE

1. To express possession:

> **le nom de l'ami** *the friend's name*
> **le stylo du garçon** *the boy's (fountain) pen*

2. To express parts of the body:

> **j'ai levé la main** *I raised my hand*
> **j'ai mal à la tête** *I have a pain in my head = I have a headache*

3. Before the names of most countries (see list pp. 80–81).

4. Before the names of seasons:

> **C'était le printemps** *It was spring*

But not after **en** *in*: **en été** *in (the) summer*.

No article before:

cent *a hundred*   **mille** *a thousand*.
Names of most towns and cities: **Londres** *London*, **Paris** *Paris*.
Some words preceded by **avec** *with*, **de** meaning *made of*, **en** *in*, **par** *by*.

Examples: **cent francs** *a (one) hundred francs*
avec plaisir *with pleasure*
une chaise de bois *a chair made of wood = a wooden chair*
je l'ai appris par cœur *I learnt it by heart*

Article and gender of nouns

Because all French nouns are either of masculine or of feminine gender, whether animate or inanimate, it is advisable to learn an article with each noun as it is met: **un avion** *an aeroplane*. **la table** *the table*.

NOUNS

Nouns are words which name animate beings, inanimate things, or abstract ideas.

GENDER

All French nouns are either masculine or feminine in gender, which does not mean that these terms are equivalent to English ideas of male and female. Masculine and feminine gender in French are merely convenient terms in grammar.

The gender of a French noun is best learnt by memorizing with it an article which indicates its gender: **un homme** (*a*) *man*, **un avion** (*an*) *aeroplane*, **le monde** (*the*) *world*, **un arbre** (*a*) *tree*, **la peur** (*the*) *fear*, **la peinture** (*the*) *painting*. One can often get an idea of French gender from (*a*) meaning, and (*b*) ending. Thus: male human beings and animals are masculine, female human beings and animals are feminine; words ending in **-tion** are all feminine. The following pointers will help:

Masculine are:	Feminine are:
Months, days of the week, seasons, colours, metals, trees. Most countries and rivers not ending in **-e**. Names of languages. The whole metric system. Most nouns ending **-age, -isme, -eau, -ent**.	Most names of countries ending **-e**. Flowers, fruits, vegetables ending in **-e**. Most abstract nouns ending **-eur**. Most nouns ending in: **-aison, -ance, -ence, -anse, -ense. -ée, -ie. -té, -tie. -tion, -sion, -xion**.

Nouns of both genders:

un aide helper, assistant	**une aide** aid, help, relief
le garde guard, keeper	**la garde** guarding, watching over, the watch
le livre book	**la livre** pound (lb. or £)
le tour turn, tour, stroll	**la tour** tower
le vapeur steamer	**la vapeur** steam, vapour, mist

* **un aide** and **le garde** are used to make compounds:
  un aide-chirurgien *assistant surgeon*. **un garde-boue** *mudguard*.

Note: **un enfant** *child* may be either m or f according to sex, but the plural is always m: **Ma chère enfant**, but **mes chers enfants**.

FEMININE OF NOUNS

The feminine of nouns is often formed by adding **e**-mute to the masculine:

> **le marchand** *shopkeeper, tradesman*
> **la marchande** *shopkeeper* (f), *tradeswoman*
> **le boucher** *butcher* (m)
> **la bouchère** (f)

Masculine nouns ending in **-eur** change this ending to **-euse** in the feminine:

> **le blanchisseur** *laundryman*
> **la blanchisseuse** *laundrywoman, washerwoman*

Masculine nouns ending in **-n** double the **n** and add **-e**:

> **le patron** *owner* (*of a business*), *employer, boss*
> **la patronne** *owner* (f)
> **le chien** *dog*
> **la chienne** *bitch*

Some nouns ending in **-e** do not change in form:

> **le** or **la concierge** *caretaker*
> **un artiste** *artist, actor*   **une artiste** *actress*
> **un Belge, une Belge** *a Belgian*
> **un, une Russe** *a Russian*
> **un, une élève** *a pupil*
> **un, une malade** *a sick person, invalid*

The article indicates the gender in such nouns.
Nouns with a different word for each gender:

le père *father*	**la mère** *mother*
le mari *husband*	**la femme** *wife* (also *woman*)
un homme *man*	**une femme** *woman*
le garçon *boy*	**la fille** *girl*
le fils *son*	**la fille** *daughter*
le frère *brother*	**la sœur** *sister*
un oncle *uncle*	**une tante** *an aunt*
le coq *cock*	**la poule** *hen*
le bœuf (pl -s) *bullock*, *ox*	**la vache** *cow*
le mouton *sheep*	**la brebis** *ewe*
le cheval *horse*	**la jument** *mare*

PLURAL OF NOUNS

General rule: The plural of a noun is generally formed by adding **-s** to the singular: **le livre** *book*; **les livres** *books*.
Exceptions:

1. Nouns ending in **-s, -x, -z** do not change: **le fils** *son*; **les fils** *sons*. **le nez** *nose*; **les nez** *noses*. **la croix** *cross*; **les croix** *crosses*.

2. Singular nouns ending in **-au, -eu** add **-x** to form the plural: **le bateau** *boat*; **les bateaux**. **le neveu** *nephew*; **les neveux**. Also some ending in **-ou** add **-x**: **le bijou** *jewel*; **les bijoux**. **le chou** *cabbage*; **les choux**. **le genou** *knee*; **les genoux**. (Most **-ou** nouns take **-s**).

3. Most singular nouns ending in **-al, -ail** change these endings to **-aux** in the plural: **le cheval** *horse*; **les chevaux**. **le travail** *work*; **les travaux**.

But note: **le bal** *ball, dance*; **les bals**. **le carnaval** *carnival*; **les carnavals**.

4. Other parts of speech used as nouns form their plurals regularly: **le baiser** *kiss*; **les baisers**. **le déjeuner** *breakfast*; **les déjeuners**. (Infinitives used as nouns are always masculine.) **Monsieur** *sir, Mr*; **messieurs**. **mademoiselle** *Miss*; **mesdemoiselles**. **madame** *Mrs*; **mesdames**.

COMPOUND NOUNS

Some compound nouns are written as one word, and then they form their plurals as above: **portemanteau**; pl **portemanteaux**. **contrevent** *shutter*; **contrevents** *shutters*.

The rules for forming the plural of compound nouns not written as one word are complex and not always logical. It is best to memorize such nouns as they are met. But note these:

Singular	Plural
le chef-d'œuvre *masterpiece*	**les chefs-d'œuvre**
la garde-robe *wardrobe*	**les garde-robes**
le (la) garde-malade *nurse*	**les gardes-malades**
le grand-père *grandfather*	**les grands-pères**
la grand'mère *grandmother*	**les grand'mères**
un hors-d'œuvre	**des hors-d'œuvre**
un après-midi *afternoon*	**des après-midi**

Final note on nouns: Consult the French-English Vocabulary at the end of the book (or a good dictionary) for other variants or irregularities in the formation of feminine or plural of nouns. Also see under Adjectives, pp. 21–27.

ADJECTIVES

An adjective is a word added to a noun to describe it more fully. There are various kinds of adjectives, which will be duly dealt with in turn. The commonest are:

QUALIFYING ADJECTIVES

Agreement of adjective with noun

In French, the adjective has a masculine and a feminine form, and each of these forms has a plural, which ends in -s. The adjective agrees in gender and number with its noun. Thus:

le petit livre *the little book*   **la petite chose** *the little thing*
les petits livres *the little books*   **les petites choses** *the little things*

Feminine form of adjectives

This is usually made by adding -e to the masculine form, as in **petit, petite.** But there are other ways of forming the feminine, of which the following must be noted:

-eau	-elle	**beau, belle** *beautiful*
-eur	-euse	**voleur, -euse** *thief*
-eux	-euse	**heureux, -euse** *happy*
-er	-ère	**étranger, étrangère** *foreign, foreigner*
-oux	-ouse	**jaloux, -ouse** *jealous*
-c	-que	**public, publique** *public*
-f	-ve	**bref, brève** *short, brief*
-g	-gue	**long, longue** *long*
-l ⎫	Double the last	**cruel, cruelle** *cruel*
-n ⎬	consonant and	**bon, bonne** *good*
-s ⎨	add -e-mute to	**gros, grosse** *fat, stout*
-t ⎭	masc	**muet, muette** *deaf*

A few words ending in -et form feminines in -ète:

complet	complète *complete*
discret	discrète *discreet*
inquiet	inquiète *uneasy, worried*
secret	secrète *secret*

Irregular feminines:

blanc	blanche *white*
franc	franche *frank, sincere*
frais	fraîche *cool, fresh*
faux	fausse *false, erroneous*
sec	sèche *dry*
acteur	actrice *actor, actress*

Dual masculine forms:

normal masc	dual form*	feminine
beau	bel	belle *beautiful*
fou	fol	folle *mad, crazy*
nouveau	nouvel	nouvelle *new*
mou	mol	molle *soft*
vieux	vieil	vieille *old*

* This dual form is used before masculine nouns beginning with a vowel or h-mute: **un bel homme** *a handsome man*, **un fol enfant** *a silly child*, **le nouvel an** *the new year*, **un mol** édredon *a soft eiderdown*.

Plural of adjectives ending in -s or -x

If the adjective ends in -s or -x it remains unchanged in the masculine plural, but in the feminine plural adds -s to that form. Thus:

ms **heureux**   mpl **heureux**   fs **heureuse**   fpl **heureuses**

Position of the adjective

In general, the adjective follows the noun in French, especially when it describes some physical, external or merely accidental quality. The natural place for the adjective is after the noun:

un chapeau noir *a black hat*
le drapeau rouge *the red flag*
l'Académie française *the French Academy*

un bateau blanc *a white boat*
un fruit amer *a bitter fruit*
une pomme amère *a bitter apple*

Adjectives placed before the noun

	ms	mpl	fs	fpl
beautiful	beau	beaux	belle	belles
good	bon	bons	bonne	bonnes
dear	cher	chers	chère	chères
nice	gentil	gentils	gentille	gentilles
big	grand	grands	grande	grandes
young	jeune	jeunes	jeune	jeunes
pretty	joli	jolis	jolie	jolies
long	long	longs	longue	longues
bad	mauvais	mauvais	mauvaise	mauvaises
better	meilleur	meilleurs	meilleure	meilleures
new	nouveau	nouveaux	nouvelle	nouvelles
little	petit	petits	petite	petites
old	vieux	vieux	vieille	vieilles

Adjectives which change in meaning according to position

bon	un bon garçon *a good sort*	un garçon bon *a kind boy*
brave	un brave homme *an honest man*	un homme brave *a brave man*
grand	un grand homme *a great man*	un homme grand *a tall man*
certain	un certain mal *some evil*	un mal certain *a positive evil*
cher	un cher livre *a favourite book*	un livre cher *an expensive book*
dernier	la dernière année *the last year*	l'année dernière *last year*

Degrees of comparison

1. Superiority:

plus + (adjective) +	**que**	
more + (adjective) +	*than*	
plus	rouge	que (l'autre)
more	*red* (=*redder*)	*than* (*the other one*)

2. Inferiority:

moins + (adjective) + **que**		
less + (adjective) + *than*		
moins	rouge	que
less	*red*	*than*

3. Equality:

> aussi + (adjective) + que
> *as* + (adjective) + *as*
> **aussi   bleu   que**
> *as   blue   as*

Very is translated by **très** (adv) before the adjective: **fort** instead of **très** is a little stronger. Thus:

> **Je suis très content** *I am very pleased*
> **Elle est fort contente** *She is extremely pleased*

The superlative

When no comparison is made, use one of the adverbs **très, fort, bien** or **extrêmement** (*extremely*):

> **Elle a été extrêmement malade** *She has been extremely ill*

When a comparison is made, and the highest or lowest degree has to be expressed, use **le, la, les plus,** or **le, la, les moins** (*the most, the least*) + the adjective. Thus:

> **le plus grand** *the tallest*
> **la plus petite** *the smallest*
> **la moins difficile** *the least difficult*
> **les plus belles femmes** *the most beautiful women*

In after a superlative is translated by **de**:

> **Ma mère était la plus belle femme de la ville** *My mother was the most beautiful woman of the town* (= *in the town*)

Irregular comparatives

bon *good*	**meilleur** *better*	**le meilleur** *the best*
mauvais *bad*	*plus mauvais or **pire**	*le plus mauvais or le pire
petit *small*	*plus petit or **moindre**	*le plus petit or le moindre

* Use **plus mauvais, le plus mauvais** and **plus petit, le plus petit. Moindre** is seldom heard in everyday speech, but may be met in writing.

POSSESSIVE ADJECTIVES

Pronouns See p. 40	je *I*	tu *thou*	il *he* elle *she*
Possessives: m	mon *my*	ton *thy*	son *his, her, its*
fem	ma	ta	sa
Pl m & f	mes	tes	ses

Pronouns See p. 40	nous *we*	vous *you*	ils *they* (m) elles *they* (f)
Possessives: m	notre *our*	votre *your*	leur *their*
fem	notre	votre	leur
Pl m & f	nos	vos	leurs

These words, placed before the noun, indicate to whom the person or thing belongs and, like all adjectives in French, agree in gender and number with the noun. Thus:

mon crayon *my pencil*	**son crayon** *his or her pencil*
ma plume *my pen*	**sa plume** *his or her pen*
mes livres *my books*	**ses livres** *his or her books*

Note that, unlike English, the gender of the person who owns the thing is irrelevant. **Notre, votre** and **leur** are used for both genders. **Leur** has **-s** before a plural noun:

leurs livres *their* (m & f) *books*

The masculine forms **mon, ton, son** must be used before feminine nouns beginning with a vowel or **h**-mute:

mon amie (f) *my girl friend*
ton adresse (f) *your (fam) address*
son aile (f) *its wing (of bird or aeroplane)*

DEMONSTRATIVE ADJECTIVES

	masc sing	fem sing	plural both genders
	ce *this, that*	**cette** *this, that*	**ces** *these, those*
Before a vowel and **h**-mute	**cet** *this, that*	**cette** *this, that*	**ces** *these, those*

They all mean both *this* and *that* and no distinction is made in

French unless one wishes to emphasize one or the other. Then one
adds to the noun either **-ci** (adv) *here*, or **-là** (adv) *there*. Thus:

unemphatic	emphatic
ce bateau *this (that) boat*	**ce bateau-ci** *this boat*
	ce bateau-là *that boat*
cet homme *this (that) man*	**cet homme-ci** *this man*
	cet homme-là *that man*
cette femme *this (that) woman*	**cette femme-ci** *this woman*
	cette femme-là *that woman*
ces enfants *these (those) children*	**ces enfants-ci** *these children*
	ces enfants-là *those children*

INTERROGATIVE ADJECTIVES

	masc	m pl	fem	f pl
Before a noun	**quel?**	**quels?**	**quelle?**	**quelles?** *which?*

Quelle heure est-il? *What hour (= time) is it?*
Quel livre désirez-vous? *Which book do you want?*
Quels chiens sont là? *Which dogs are (over) there?*
Quelle maison préférez-vous? *Which house do you prefer?*
Quelles leçons avons-nous
   aujourd'hui? *What lessons have we today?*

INDEFINITE ADJECTIVES

These indicate that the noun is used in a general way that may sometimes be vague. They always precede the noun. Those given below
are the commonest in use:

autre (m & f), **autres** (pl) *other, others* — **un autre homme** *another man*
certain, certains; certaine, certaines (precedes noun) *some, certain* — **certaines personnes** *some people*
chaque (inv) *each, every* — **chaque jour** *every day, each day*
même, mêmes (m & f) *same* — **la même chose** *the same thing*
plusieurs (inv) *several* — **plusieurs personnes** *several persons*
quelque, quelques *some* — **quelque chose** *something*
tel, tels; telle, telles *such* — **un tel homme** *such a man*
une telle femme *such a woman*

tout, tous; toute, toutes *all, the whole, every*

> **tout le pain** *all the bread*
> **toute la viande** *all the meat*
> **lisez toute la lettre** *read the whole letter*

Note: Do not confuse any of these with similar indefinite pronouns (p. 43). Adjectives always go with a noun, and pronouns replace a noun or pronoun.

NUMERAL WORDS

CARDINAL NUMBERS

1 **un, une** *one*
2 **deux** *two*
3 **trois** *three*
4 **quatre** *four*
5 **cinq** *five**
6 **six** *six* (pr x as -ss*)
7 **sept** *seven*
8 **huit** *eight*
9 **neuf** *nine*
10 **dix** *ten* (pr x as -ss*)
11 **onze** *eleven*
12 **douze** *twelve*
13 **treize** *thirteen*
14 **quatorze** *fourteen*
15 **quinze** *fifteen*
16 **seize** *sixteen*
17 **dix-sept** *seventeen*
18 **dix-huit** *eighteen*
19 **dix-neuf** *nineteen*
20 **vingt** *twenty*
21 **vingt et un** *twenty-one*
22 **vingt-deux** *twenty-two*
23 **vingt-trois** *twenty-three*
24 **vingt-quatre** *twenty-four*
25 **vingt-cinq** *twenty-five*
26 **vingt-six** *twenty-six*
27 **vingt-sept** *twenty-seven*
28 **vingt-huit** *twenty-eight*
29 **vingt-neuf** *twenty-nine*
30 **trente** *thirty*
31, 32, etc. **trente et un, trente-deux,** etc.
40 **quarante** *forty*
50 **cinquante** *fifty*
60 **soixante** *sixty* (pr x as -ss-)
70 **soixante-dix** *seventy*
71 **soixante et onze** *seventy-one*

77 **soixante-dix-sept** *seventy-seven*
80 **quatre-vingts** *eighty*
81 **quatre-vingt-un** *eighty-one*
90 **quatre-vingt-dix** *ninety*
91 **quatre-vingt-onze** *ninety-one*
97 **quatre-vingt-dix-sept** *ninety-seven*
100 **cent** *a hundred*
101 **cent un** *a hundred and one*
102 **cent deux,** etc. *a hundred and two,* etc.
200 **deux cents** *two hundred*
201 **deux cent un** *two hundred and one*
202 **deux cent deux,** etc.
300 **trois cents** *three hundred*
301 **trois cent un** *three hundred and one*
302 **trois cent deux,** etc.
400 **quatre cents** *four hundred*
500 **cinq cents** *five hundred*
600 **six cents** *six hundred*
700 **sept cents** *seven hundred*
800 **huit cents** *eight hundred*
900 **neuf cents** *nine hundred*
1000 **mille** *a thousand* Mil = 1000 in dates only
2000 **deux mille** *two thousand*
1 000 000 **un million** *a million*
2 000 000 **deux millions** *two million*
1 000 000 000 **un milliard** *a milliard* or *one thousand million*
2 000 000 000 **deux milliards** *two milliard* or *two thousand million*

* The q in **cinq** and the x in **six** and **dix** are pronounced only when the number stands by itself, e.g. **j'en ai six** *I have six of them* and not when it is followed by a noun, e.g. **dix personnes**.

Decimals

Where the English use a decimal point, the French use a decimal comma. Thus:

> English 1·005 (*one point nought nought five*)
> French **1,005** (un virgule zéro zéro cinq)

Where the comma is used in English to separate sets of three figures, the French use either a space or a point. The preference is now for the space. Thus:

> English *1,000,000 one million*
> French **1 000 000** or **1.000.000 un million**

Note: The figure 1 is usually written with an upstroke, thus 1 or 1. As a consequence, the figure 7 in France is crossed, thus 7, as otherwise it might be confused with a 1 (one).

ORDINAL NUMBERS

1st	**1er/ère**	**le premier, la première***
2nd	**2e**	**le (la) deuxième** (second, -e)
3rd	**3e**	**le (la) troisième**
4th	**4e**	**le (la) quatrième**
5th	**5e**	**le (la) cinquième**
6th	**6e**	**le (la) sixième**
7th	**7e**	**le (la) septième**
8th	**8e**	**le (la) huitième**
9th	**9e**	**le (la) neuvième**
10th	**10e**	**le (la) dixième**
11th	**11e**	**le (la) onz-**
12th	**12e**	**le (la) douz-**
13th	**13e**	**le (la) treiz-**
14th	**14e**	**le (la) quatorz-**
15th	**15e**	**le (la) quinz-**
16th	**16e**	**le (la) seiz-**
17th	**17e**	**le (la) dix-sept-**
18th	**18e**	**le (la) dix-huit-**
19th	**19e**	**le (la) dix-neuv-**
20th	**20e**	**le (la) vingt-**

Ordinal ending = **-ième** (for 11th–20th)

***unième** *first* in compound ordinals. Thus: **le vingt et unième, trente et unième 21e, 31e** *21st, 31st.*

quatre-vingt-unième *81st.*   quatre-vingt-onzième *91st.*
30th le (la) trentième.   *40th* quarantième.   *50th* cinquantième.
60th soixantième.   *70th* soixante-dixième.   *80th* quatre-vingtième.
90th quatre-vingt-dixième.   *100th* centième.   *101st* cent et unième.
200th deux centième.   *1000th* millième.

FRACTIONS

la moitié (de) *the half (of)*	le cinquième *the fifth*
le tiers *the third*	le vingtième *the 20th*
le quart *the quarter*	le centième *the 100th*, etc.

le (la) demi(e) is the exact or mathematical half. la moitié *half* in everyday speech. One says une bonne moitié (de) *a good half (of)*. And six heures et demie *half past six* (see also under *Time of Day*, p. 31). la demie *the half hour*. demi-cuit *half-cooked*.

'TIMES'

la fois *time, occasion*, is used to form adverbs of time. Thus:

une fois *once*	deux cents fois *two hundred times*
deux fois *twice*	mille fois *a thousand times*
trois fois *three times*	

FRENCH CARDINAL USED FOR ENGLISH ORDINAL

Except for premier, -ère, French uses a cardinal number where English often uses an ordinal:

1. After names of sovereigns:

> Henri VIII (huit) *Henry the Eighth*
> But: Henri Ier (premier)

2. In the date (see p. 31).

AGE

Quel âge avez-vous? *How old are you?*
J'ai dix-huit ans *I am eighteen (years old, years of age)*

Use avoir + cardinal number

DATE

Le combien sommes-nous? *What is the date?*
Nous sommes le 11 (onze) janvier *It is the 11th of January*
The 11th of January 1966 **le 11 janvier 1966 (mil neuf cent soixante-six)**

Note: **mil** is used for **mille** when writing the date, not otherwise.

THE TIME OF DAY

Quelle heure est-il, s'il vous plaît? *What is the time, please?*
Pouvez-vous me dire l'heure juste? *Can you tell me the correct (right) time?*

Il est une heure	*one o'clock*
une heure cinq	*1.5, five past one*
une heure dix	*1.10, ten past one*
une heure et quart	*1.15, quarter past one*
une heure vingt	*1.20, twenty past one*
une heure et demie	*1.30, half past one*
deux heures moins le quart	*1.45, quarter to two*
Il est midi	*It is noon*
Il est minuit	*It is midnight*
neuf heures du matin	*9 a.m.*
sept heures du soir	*7 p.m.*
être à l'heure	*to be on time*
être en retard	*to be late*
être en avance	*to be early*

The 24-hour clock

The transport systems (railways, buses, etc.) and official notices in France use the 24-hour system. This begins with 12 o'clock midnight as zero hour. Thus:

12-hour system	24-hour system
12.0 midnight **minuit** {	Arrival: **vingt-quatre heures:** *24 o'clock*
	Departure: **zéro heure**
12.15 a.m.	**00.15 zéro quinze**
9.30 a.m.	**09.30 neuf heures trente**
12.00 noon	**12.00 douze heures;** or **midi**
1.00 p.m.	**13.00 treize heures**
2.2 p.m.	**14.02 quatorze heures deux**
11.40 p.m.	**23.40 vingt-trois heures quarante**

Personal pronouns

1 Subject	2 Direct object	3 Indirect object	4 Reflexive	5 Disjunctive or emphatic (away from verb)
		(with the verb)		
je *I*	me *me*	me *(to) me*	me *myself*	moi
tu* *you* (fam)	te *you*	te *(to) you*	te *yourself*	toi
il *he*	le *him*	lui *(to) him*	se *himself*	lui
elle *she*	la *her*	lui *(to) her*	se *herself*	elle
nous *we*	nous *us*	nous *(to) us*	nous *ourselves*	nous
vous *you*	vous *you*	vous *(to) you*	vous *yourselves*	vous
ils *they*	les *them*	leur *(to) them*	se *themselves*	eux
elles *they*	les *them*	leur *(to) them*	se *themselves*	elles

*tu *thou*: *thou* is archaic in English but is much used in French as a familiar form for *you*. Members of the same family, friends and classmates generally use it. It can be used by the foreigner when talking to children, but not unless or until a fairly close relationship has been established. Then tu=*you*.

vous+2nd pers plural verb is normally used for *you* when there is any doubt.

There is no neutral form *it*. The English *it* has to be translated by either il or elle according to the gender of the noun.

PRONOUNS

For the personal pronouns, see table on opposite page.

Other personal pronouns are **y** and **en** (both are also adverbs, and **en** also a preposition).

As pronouns, these are used for:

y *to, at, in, by, of* + a noun or pronoun (*him, her, it,* etc.) used as predicate:

je le fais sans y penser *I do it without thinking (of it)* (*of it* = predicate)
j'y ai mis mes gants *I put my gloves in it*

en *of it, from it, some, any.* **En** avoids repetition of noun or pronouns:

Nous en parlerons *We'll speak about (of) it*
Il en partira demain *He will leave it (the place) tomorrow*
j'en ai *I have some (of it)*
je n'en ai pas *I haven't any (of it)*

soi, soi-même *one, oneself:* is used after the indefinite pronoun **on** *one, they, people.*

On pense à soi *one thinks of oneself*

même *self.* Used with all the disjunctive pronouns for emphasis:

moi-même *myself*   **lui-même** *himself*   **eux-mêmes** *themselves* (m)

POSITION OF PERSONAL PRONOUNS
WITH VERB

1, 2, 3, 4 in the Table opposite are placed before the verb, except in the imperative affirmative. Those under 5 are always placed away from the verb. Note the order of object pronouns:

Object pronouns with verb

Order	1 precedes	2 precedes	3 precedes	4 precedes	5		
	me						
Subject	te	le	lui		y	en	verb
or	se	la	leur				
pronoun	nous	les					
	vous						
	se						

Order in negative sentences, **ne** before object pronouns, then verb, then **pas**:

je ne le regarde pas

The commonest combinations are:

> me le, me la, me les, te le, te la, te les, se le, se la, se les
> nous le, nous la, nous les, vous le, vous la, vous les
> le lui, la lui, les lui, le leur, la leur, les leur
> m'en, t'en, s'en, l'en, nous en, vous en, les en
> m'y, t'y, s'y, l'y, nous y, vous y, les y

Rule: Indirect object precedes the direct, except when both pronouns are (*1*) in the third person or (*2*) after an imperative affirmative, when the direct object precedes the indirect.
Examples:

> **Je vous donne une pomme** *I give you an apple*
> **Je vous la donne** *I give it* (*the apple*) *to you*
> **Je lui parle** *I speak to him*
> **Je lui ai parlé** *I spoke to him* (*her*)
> **Je lui dit** *I tell him*
> **Je le lui dis** *I tell it to him*
> **Je le lui ai dit** *I told it to him*

Je ne le leur ai pas encore dit *I have not yet told it to them*
Il ne m'y verra pas *He will not see me there*
Il ne vous y en a pas encore envoyé *He has not sent you any there yet*

Object pronoun with the imperative

Affirmative: after the verb	Negative: before the verb
Donnez-les-moi *Give them to me*	**Ne me les donnez pas** *Don't give them to me*
Dites-le-lui *Tell it to him*	**Ne le lui dites pas** *Don't tell it to him*

Expliquez-le-leur *Explain it to them*

Parlez-lui-en *Speak to him of it*

Allez-vous-en! *Go away!*
Va-t'en! *Go away (Get out of it!)*
Allez-y! *Go to it! Go there!*
Vas-y! *Go on! Go there!*
Donnez-m'en *Give me some*

Ne le leur expliquez pas *Don't explain it to them*

Ne lui en parlez pas *Don't speak to him about it*

Ne vous en allez pas *Don't go away*
Ne t'en va pas *Don't go away*
N'y allez pas *Don't go there*
N'y va pas *Don't go there*
Ne m'en donnez pas *Don't give me any*

Interrogative sentences

Parlez-vous? *Do you speak?*   **Me parlez-vous?** *Are you speaking to me?*

Subject pronoun comes after the verb, object pronoun goes before.

REFLEXIVE PRONOUNS (4 IN TABLE p. 32)

These are used with reflexive verbs. See p. 52.

DISJUNCTIVE PERSONAL PRONOUNS

Disjunctive personal pronouns (5 in Table, p. 32) are so called because they can be used apart from the verb.

They are used as (*1*) emphatics, (*2*) alone or (*3*) after a preposition.

Qui dit ça? *Who says that?*   **Eux** *They (do)*
Lui, il dit qu'il va en France *He says that he is going to France*

The emphasis can be strengthened by the addition of another word:

Moi aussi *I also*   **Elle seule** *She alone*

Note the common addition of **-même** *-self*:

moi-même *myself*   **toi-même** *yourself* (fam)
lui-même *himself*   **elle-même** *herself*
nous-mêmes *ourselves*   **vous-mêmes** *yourselves*
eux-mêmes (m) *themselves* **elles-mêmes** (f) *themselves*
soi-même *himself, herself, itself, oneself*

They are used after the 3rd pers sing of **être** as complement in such statements as **C'est moi** *It is I*, **C'était lui** *It was he*. (See p. 38 for **c'est** and **il est**.)

After **que** *than* in comparative statements:

>   **Jean est plus âgé que moi** *John is older than me*

Note that **soi** (reflexive) is used as a disjunctive pronoun after indefinites such as **on, chacun, quelqu'un, tout le monde, personne**:

>   **On décide pour soi** *One decides for oneself*
>   **Chacun pour soi** *Everybody for himself*

Disjunctive personal pronouns are often used as possessive pronouns, with the preposition **à** before them. Thus:

à moi *mine*	**à toi** *yours* (fam)	**à lui** *his*	**à elle** *hers*
à nous *ours*	**à vous** *yours*	**à eux** (m), **à elles** (f) *theirs*	

>   **C'est à moi** *It is mine*
>   **À qui sont ces chapeaux?** *Whose are these hats?*
>   **Ce sont les nôtres** or **Ils sont à nous** *They are ours*

DEMONSTRATIVE PRONOUNS

There are two demonstrative pronouns: **celui** and **ce**, both meaning *this* or *that*. They draw attention to the person or thing spoken of. To clarify meaning, **-ci** (from **ici** *here*) or **-là** *there* can be added to **celui**. Thus:

	masc		fem		
Singular:	**celui-ci** *this (one)*	**celle-ci**	**ceci** *this*	**ce, c'** *this, that, it*
	celui-là *that (one)*	**celle-là**	**cela (ça)** *that*	(impers)
Plural:	**ceux-ci** *these*	**celles-ci**	—	**ce** *they, these*
	ceux-là *those*	**celles-là**		(impers)

Agreement: **celui** changes form to agree in gender and number with the noun to which it refers:

Mon crayon est noir, celui de ma sœur est bleu	*My pencil is black, that of my sister (my sister's) is blue*
Voici mes plumes et celles de mon frère	*Here are my pens and those of my brother (my brother's)*

Celui+qui: When **celui** is followed by the relative pronoun **qui** (see p. 41) it means *he, she, him, her, the one who*:

>   **Celui qui vous parle** *He (or the one or the man) who speaks to you*
>   **le crayon de Jean**   **celui de Jean**

la gomme de Jean	celle de Jean	Note the agreements
les crayons de Jean	ceux de Jean	
les gommes de Jean	celles de Jean	

Jean est le garçon qui entre, et celui qui sort aussi
Marie est la jeune fille qui entre, et celle qui sort aussi
Jean et Paul sont les garçons qui entrent, et ceux qui sortent aussi
Marie et Helène sont les jeunes filles qui entrent, et celles qui sortent aussi

THE 'NEUTERS'

| ceci *this* | ce *this* | c'est *it is* | est-ce? *is it?* |
| cela *that* | ça *that* | ce sont *they are* | sont-ce? *are they?* |

Ceci (like **celui-ci**) is used when speaking of the nearby, and **cela** (like **celui-là**) is used when referring to something away from the speaker. But, whereas **celui-ci** and **celui-là** are used of persons and things, *ceci* and *cela*, if for persons, should be used only when speaking familiarly or with contempt. **Ça**=**cela**. (**Çà**=*here*, as in *çà et là here and there*.) It is best for the foreigner to use **ceci** and **cela** for things or ideas. Thus:

> **Il ne faut pas oublier cela** *That must not be forgotten*
> **Cela m'est égal** (coll and fam **ça m'est égal**) *It's (all) the same to me*
> **N'oubliez pas ceci** *Don't forget it (the last thing spoken of)*

When in doubt, use **cela**:

> **cela se comprend** *that's understood*

Ce as a pronoun may be regarded as (mostly) neuter, though it can stand for all genders. It has only the forms **ce** and **c'**. **ce qui** and **ce que** *that (thing) which; what*. Thus:

> **ce qui est arrivé** *that which happened*
> **ce que je dis** *what I am saying*

With the verbs **être** *to be*, **pouvoir** *to be able*, **devoir** *to have to*, and **sembler** *to seem*, **ce** is used with the third person singular to make impersonal statements. Thus:

> **Ce doit être lui** *It must be he*
> **Ce peut être elle** *It can (may) be her*
> **Ce semble être Jean** *It seems to be John*
> **Ce lui sera un plaisir** *It will be a pleasure to him*

It can be used for persons and things:

C'est Jean *It's John* **C'est lui** *It's he* **Ce n'est pas vrai** *It's not true*

The use of *ce* and *il*: *c'est* and *il est*

Ce, c' is a demonstrative pronoun meaning *it* or *that*, often in an impersonal sense. Thus it usually refers to something already in mind.

c'est *it is*   **ce sont** *they are*

il is a personal pronoun, often translated by *it*, impersonal. Otherwise it refers to a masculine noun.

Use **il est**

1. before a masc noun without an article denoting status, calling, profession, occupation or a noun of nationality:

> **Il est médecin** *He is a doctor*
> **Il est curé** *He's a parish priest*
> **Il est veuf** *He is a widower*
> **Il est Américain** *He is an American*

2. before a masc adjective:

> **Il est fameux** *He/it is famous*
> **Il est heureux** *He is happy*

3. impersonally, when it refers to what follows:

> **Il est mieux de ne pas y aller** *It is better not to go there*

4. before the time of day, unqualified:

> **Il est une heure** *It is one o'clock*
> **Il est six heures** *It is six o'clock*
> (See p. 31)

5. in impersonal statements such as

> **Il est vrai que . . .** *It is true that . . .*
> **Il est difficile de . . .** *It is difficult to . . .*

(Note that adjectives are mostly used in such statements.)

Use **ce, c', ce sont**

1. when followed by a noun with an article or a possessive pronoun, or the name of a person:

> **C'est un homme** *It is a man, that is a man*
> pl **Ce sont des hommes** *They are men*
> **C'est ma sœur** *It is (she is) my sister*
> **Ce sont mes frères** *It is (they are) my brothers*
> **C'est Charles** *It is Charles*
> **C'est Dupont** *It is Dupont*

2. when followed by a disjunctive pronoun:

> **C'est moi** *It is I*
> **Ce sont eux** *It is they*

3. in **c'est à** + an infinitive:

> **C'est à éviter** *It is (something) to be avoided*

4. **c'est** can be used to emphasize almost anything that follows it:

C'est avec Jean que je désire aller à Londres *It is with John (that) I wish to go to London*
C'est à Paris que je veux aller *It is to Paris that I want to go*

Common phrases with **ce**:

Est-ce que ...? *Is it that ...?* placed before any affirmative statement makes it interrogative:

> **Vous allez à Paris** *You are going to Paris*
> **Est-ce que vous allez à Paris?** *Are you going to Paris?*

c'est que *it is because*, usually preceded by a clause:

S'il ne vient pas, c'est qu'il est malade *If he does not come, it is because he is ill*

c'est-à-dire *that is to say*:

J'irai à Paris — c'est-à-dire si j'ai l'argent *I will go to Paris—that is (to say) if I have the money*

POSSESSIVE PRONOUNS

Compare these with the possessive adjectives on p. 25. The forms for possessive pronouns are old stressed forms of possessive adjectives.

Possessive pronouns are preceded by the appropriate article. They replace a noun already expressed and denote possession:

Possessive adjective:	*Voici mon chapeau*	**Here is my hat**
Possessive pronoun:	*Voici le mien*	**Here is mine**

Forms of possessive pronouns

One possessor

Person:	**je**	**tu**	**il, elle**
S: m:	**le mien**	**le tien**	**le sien**
f:	**la mienne**	**la tienne**	**la sienne**
Pl: m:	**les miens**	**les tiens**	**les siens**
f:	**les miennes**	**les tiennes**	**les siennes**
	mine	*thine*	*his, hers, its*
		(= *yours* fam)	

More than one possessor

Person:	**nous**	**vous**	**ils, elles**
S: m:	**le**	**le**	**le**
f:	**la** nôtre	**la** vôtre	**la** leur
Pl: m:	**les**	**les**	**les**
f:	**les** nôtres	**les** vôtres	**les** leurs
	ours	*yours*	*theirs*

Agreement: The possessive pronoun agrees in gender and number with the object possessed. Thus:

J'ai perdu ma montre, prête-moi la tienne *I have lost my watch, lend me yours* (fam)

J'ai perdu mon stylo, mais elle m'a donné le sien *I lost my fountain pen, but she gave me hers*

Ces chapeaux sont les nôtres *These hats are ours*

But see p. 36 for the use of disjunctives as possessive pronouns, a more common usage.

RELATIVE PRONOUNS

A relative pronoun is one which connects the noun or pronoun to which it refers with the part of the sentence which follows. Thus: *the man whom I know; the house that Jack built; the man of whom I speak. Whom* and *that* are relative pronouns. Relative pronouns are never omitted in French.

Simple relative pronouns

masc/fem   masc/fem

Subject pronoun: **qui** *who, which*   Noun-object pron: **dont** *whose,*
Object direct: **que** *whom, which*   *of whom, of which*
       indirect: **(à) qui** *to whom,*   Place-object pron: **où** *where*
                              to which

Examples of use:

C'est l'ami qui est venu hier *It is the friend who came yesterday*
C'est le livre que j'ai écrit *It is the book (that) I wrote*
Le monsieur à qui appartient cette maison est absent *The gentleman to whom this house belongs is away*
Voici la jeune fille dont je vous ai parlé *Here is the (young) girl of whom I spoke to you*
Voilà la maison où j'habite *There is the house in which I live*

Other relative pronouns:

à qui *to whom* (of persons only)
de qui *of whom* (of persons only)
de quoi *of what* (of things only)
à quoi *to what* (of things only)

Examples:

Quoi = **quelle chose?** and can also be used as exclamation
Quoi? Vous n'êtes pas parti? *What! You haven't left?*
C'est à quoi je pense *It is what I am thinking of*
De quoi parlez-vous? *What are you speaking of?*
Je ne sais pas de quoi vous parlez *I do not know what you are speaking of*

Note: The relative pronouns are also used as interrogatives, see p. 42.

The relative pronoun is never omitted in French, though it often is in English:

La maison que j'ai vendue *The house I sold*
Voici l'automobile qui me plaît *Here is the car I like*

The word (usually a noun) represented by the relative pronoun is called the antecedent. In the two examples above, **la maison** and **l'automobile** are antecedents of the relatives **que** and **qui**. **Que** is direct object relative, **qui** is subject relative.

Compound relative pronouns

	Sing		Plural	
masc	fem		masc	fem
lequel	**laquelle**		**lesquels**	**lesquelles**
duquel	**de laquelle**		**desquels**	**desquelles**
auquel	**à laquelle**		**auxquels**	**auxquelles**

1) **lequel, laquelle** *which, that 2)* **duquel, de laquelle** *of, from which*
3) **auquel, à laquelle** *to which*

Use of compound relatives: more often for things than persons. With a little ingenuity the foreigner may avoid using them altogether, relying entirely on **qui, que, à qui, dont** and **où**. But he must be able to recognize them in reading, and know their meaning. One finds in common usage a preposition + **lequel** in such sentences as:

La porte par laquelle on entre *The door by which people go in*
Il a vendu le cheval avec lequel il est venu *He sold the horse with (on) which he came*
la table sur laquelle j'écris *the table on which I write*
les idées auxquelles je pense *the ideas of which I am thinking*
le livre duquel je parle *the book of which I am speaking*

INTERROGATIVE PRONOUNS

All relative pronouns except **dont** can be used as interrogatives. But note: **quoi?** *what?* (referring to things only) **quoi de mieux?** *what better?* **à quoi?** *to what?* **de quoi?** *of what?* **avec quoi?** *with what?* **sur quoi?** *on what?* And as exclamatory **Quoi!** *What!*

> **À quoi pensez-vous?** *What are you thinking of?*
> **De quoi parlez-vous?** *What are you speaking of?*
> **Sur quoi vous basez-vous?** *On what do you base yourself?*
> **Avec quoi faites-vous ça?** *What do you do that with?*
> **À quoi bon faire ça?** *What is the good of doing that?*

> masc **quel**   fem **quelle**   *which? what?*
> pl **quels**   pl **quelles**

Quel interrogatives agree with the noun to which they refer in gender and number:

> Statement: **J'ai des nouvelles pour vous** *I have (some) news for you*
> Question: **Quelles sont-elles?** *What are they? (What is it?)*

> Qui? Qui est-ce qui ...? Subject (persons) *Who?*
> Qu'est-ce qui ...? Subject (things) *What?*
> Qui (or Qui est-ce qui) est là? *Who is there?*
> Qu'est-ce qui est tombé? *What has fallen?*

Direct object:

qui (for persons)	Qui a-t-il vu? *Whom has he seen?*
que (for things)	Qu'a-t-il vu? *What has he seen?*
avec qui? *with whom?*	avec quoi *with what?* pourquoi? *why?*

Compound relatives are used as interrogatives for the question *which?* = *which one?* or *which ones?*

> Lequel préférez-vous? *Which one do you prefer?*
> Lesquelles? (fpl) *Which ones?*

These are used when a choice is offered among a number:

> Duquel parlez-vous? *Which (one of several) are you speaking of?*

Dont is never used as interrogative:

> De qui parlez-vous? *Of whom are you speaking?*

INDEFINITE PRONOUNS

on *one, they, people* is used with the third person singular of verbs to form useful impersonal expressions:

> On dit que ... *It is said that ... People say that ...*
> On nous l'a dit *Someone told us so* (= *We were told so*)

personne *nobody*:

> Personne ne me l'a dit *Nobody told me so*
> Qui est là? Personne *Who is there? Nobody*

rien *nothing*:

> Cela ne fait rien *That makes nothing* (= *That does not matter*)
> Que voyez-vous? Rien *What do you see? Nothing*

chacun, chacune *each one*:

> chacun travaille pour soi *each one* (*everyone*) *works for himself*

quelque chose (indef pron) *something*
quiconque *whoever*
autrui *others*

All the above are invariable.

The following are variable for gender and number:

l'un l'autre *one another*   **l'un et l'autre** *both*
l'un ou l'autre *either*   **ni l'un ni l'autre** *neither*
quelqu'un *somebody*

>   **l'une l'autre.   les uns les autres.   les unes les autres.**
>   **quelqu'une.   quelques-uns.   quelques-unes.**

Note: Some indefinite adjectives (see p. 26) may be used without a noun, and then they become indefinite pronouns (**plusieurs, tout** and, in the plural, **certains** = **quelques-uns**). **Tous** as indefinite pronoun = *all*, and then the final **-s** is pronounced.

VERBS

———◆———

Verbs are words which express the happening of an action or the existence of a state. Thus: *to run, to be*: *run* and *be* are verbs.

The treatment of French verbs given here is calculated to provide those basic elements in verbs which are sufficient for most everyday purposes—and a little more.

BASIC PARTS OF VERBS WHICH MUST BE KNOWN

1. Infinitive: the part which names the action or state without reference to a specific time, person or number, as in *to run* or *to be*. Thus: **parler** *to speak*; **finir** *to finish*; **recevoir** *to receive*; **rompre** *to break*. The infinitive of a French verb has one of these four endings:

-er (the commonest), **-ir, -oir, -re**

2. Present participle: the French form, ending in **-ant**, denotes a contemporary action or state, and corresponds more or less to the English form ending in *-ing*, as in *speaking* **parlant**. And so: **finissant** *finishing*; **recevant** *receiving*; **rompant** *breaking*. All present participles end in **-ant**.

3. Present tense: denotes an action or state in the present time, and is in English expressed in three ways, as in: *I speak, I am speaking, I do speak*, all of which have only one equivalent in French: **je parle** *I speak*, etc.; **je finis** *I finish*, etc.; **je reçois** *I receive*, etc.; **je prends** *I take*, etc.

4. Future tense: denotes an action or state in the future. It is formed by adding the following endings to the infinitive of the verb:

+ -ai, -as, -a, -ons, -ez, -ont

je **parlerai** *I shall speak*
tu **parleras** *you* (fam) *will speak*
il
elle } **parlera** *he, she will speak*
nous **parlerons** *we shall speak*
vous **parlerez** *you will speak*
ils
elles } **parleront** *they will speak*

French future tense
always refers to the
future, not to a wish
or will to future

Note: I shall speak tomorrow je **parlerai** demain
I will/want to/intend to speak tomorrow je **veux parler** demain (not a
future but an intention or wish)

5. Compound past tense: so called because it is made with an
auxiliary verb + the past participle of the main verb. **Avoir** *to have*,
and **être** *to be* (see p. 48), are auxiliaries. Past participle of **parler** is
parlé. So, **j'ai parlé** *I have spoken*; **vous avez parlé** *you have spoken*,
or *you spoke*.

Note: The French compound past is in everyday use for both the
English forms: *I have spoken* and *I spoke*.

CLASSIFICATION OF FRENCH VERBS

All French verbs can be classified into three groups:

Group I

Infinitive in **-er**; present participle in **-ant**; present tense with endings
-e, -es, -e, -ons, -ez, -ent; past participle **-é**.

Example: **parler** *to speak*.

The above endings are added to the stem* of the verb.

* Stem: this is mostly found by dropping the **-ant** ending of the present participle:
parlant; stem = **parl-**.

Present tense:

je **parle** *I speak*   nous **parlons** *we speak*
tu **parles** *you* (fam) *speak* vous **parlez** *you speak*
il   ils
elle **parle** *he she speaks*   elles **parlent** *they speak*
                                         (**-ent** silent)

Compound past tense: auxiliary + past participle:

j'ai parlé *I have spoken, I spoke*

For auxiliaries, see p. 48.

Future tense: formed by adding **-ai, -as, -a, -ons, -ez, -ont** to the infinitive:

je parlerai, etc.

Over 90 per cent of French verbs are in this group.

Group II

Infinitive **-ir**; present participle **-(i)ssant**; present tense **-s, -s, -t, -ons, -ez, -ent**.

Example: **finir** *to finish*: present participle **finissant**; stem **finiss-**.

Present tense:

	je finis *I finish*	nous finissons *we finish*	
	tu finis *you finish*	vous finissez *you finish*	
-ss- omitted	il	ils	
	elle finit *he/she finishes*	elles finissent *they finish*	
		(**-ent** silent)	

Compound past tense:

j'ai fini, tu as fini, etc. *I finished, you finished,* etc.

Future tense: infinitive + endings **-ai, -as, -a, -ons, -ez, ont**:

je finirai	nous finirons
tu finiras	vous finirez
il, elle finira	ils, elles finiront

A (limited) number of **-ir** verbs are conjugated in this way, which is regarded as 'regular' for **-ir** verbs. All other **-ir** verbs are relegated to Group III, below. The vocabulary at the end of the book marks verbs which take in **-ss-**.

See page 56 for Model Conjugations of Groups I and II verbs.

Group III

All verbs which do not fall into Groups I and II are regarded as 'irregular', though some of them have many inflexions similar to those of I or II.

Infinitives of Group III verbs have endings **-ir**, **-oir** and **-re**.

All Group III (i.e. irregular) verbs required in this book, that is, for most practical purposes, are given with their basic tenses on pp. 57–63. These must be memorized.

For reference: endings of tenses not given above

Past historic I	II	Imperfect	Conditional	Pres subj	Imp subj	Imperative
-ai	is	-ais	infinitive + imperfect	-e	-sse	—
-as	is	-ais	endings	-es	-sses	-e or s (Groups II & III)
-a	it	-ait		-e	-ˆt	—
-âmes	îmes	-ions		-ions	-ssions	-ons
-âtes	îtes	-iez		-iez	-ssiez	-ez
-èrent	irent	-aient*		-ent*	-ssent*	—

* The 3rd person plural ending in **-ent** is always silent; also final **-e**, **-es**.

A full and detailed statement of this classification, with a very much fuller list of Group III verbs, will be found in *Everyman's French–English and English–French Dictionary*, pp. xiii–xxii, by Jean-Paul Vinay and collaborators. What is given above is a simplification and adaptation for the purpose here.

AUXILIARY VERBS avoir *to have* AND être *to be* (BOTH GROUP III)

The parts of these two important verbs which are printed here must be known. They are irregular verbs and, as they are in constant use, the basic tenses should be mastered before proceeding to other verbs.

1. Present participles:

       ayant *having*   **étant** *being*

2. Past participles:

       eu *had*   **été** *been*

3. Present tense:

avoir	être
j'ai *I have*	**je suis** *I am*
tu as *you* (fam) *have*	**tu es** *you* (fam) *are*
il, elle a *he, she has*	**il, elle est** *he, she is*
nous avons *we have*	**nous sommes** *we are*
vous avez *you have*	**vous êtes** *you are*
ils, elles ont *they* (m & f) *have*	**ils, elles sont** *they* (m & f) *are*

4. Compound past tense = present tense + past participle:

j'ai eu *I have had, had*   **j'ai été** *I have been, was*, etc.

In English we say *I had, I was* far more often than we say *I have had, I have been*. The French compound past tense is the equivalent of both our English forms and is most commonly used.

5. Future tense:

j'aurai *I shall have*	**je serai** *I shall be*
tu auras *you* (fam) *will have*	**tu seras** *you* (fam) *will be*
il, elle aura *he, she will have*	**il, elle sera** *he, she will be*
nous aurons *we shall have*	**nous serons** *we shall be*
vous aurez *you will have*	**vous serez** *you will be*
ils, elles auront *they* (m & f) *will have*	**ils, elles seront** *they* (m & f) *will be*

Auxiliary verbs and compound tenses

Auxiliary verbs are used to make all compound tenses, of which the most common is the compound past. Most compound tenses are made with **avoir** *to have*. All reflexive verbs (see p. 52) are conjugated with **être**, as are most intransitive verbs of motion in their most common usage. The following, conjugated with **être**, should be memorized:

with être	**aller** *to go*	**je suis allé** *I went*
	venir *to come*	**je suis venu** *I came*
	arriver *to arrive*	**je suis arrivé** *I arrived*
	entrer *to go in*	**je suis entré** *I went in* (**dans** *into*)
	rester *to remain*	**je suis resté** *I remained*
	tomber *to fall*	**je suis tombé** *I fell*
	naître *to be born*	**je suis né** (**à Londres**) *I was born* (*in London*)
	mourir *to die*	**elle est morte** (**à Paris**) *she died* (*in Paris*)

Agreement of past participle in compound tenses

1. When a verb is conjugated with être, the past participle agrees with the subject:

> **Mon frère est arrivé** *My brother has arrived*
> **Ma sœur est arrivée** *My sister has arrived*
> **Ils sont arrivés** *They* (m) *have arrived*
> **Elles sont arrivées** *They* (f) *have arrived*

2. When **avoir** is used, the past participle agrees with the direct object if it precedes the verb:

> **j'ai vu les maisons** no agreement
> **les maisons que j'ai vues** *the houses* (which) *I saw*

3. The past participle can often be used as an adjective, and then it agrees with its noun:

Nous avons trouvé la porte ouverte *We found the door open*
J'ai reçu une lettre écrite de sa main *I received a letter written in his* (own) *hand*

THE PHRASE en train de + INFINITIVE

être en train de *to be engaged in, busy, in the act of.* Examples:

je suis en train
{ **d'étudier** *I am busy studying*
{ **d'écrire** *I am in the act of writing*
{ **de travailler** *I am engaged at work*

This is a common phrase used when one wishes to emphasize that something is being done at a given moment. In this way the normal present (or other) tense can be clarified:

Demain je serai en train de m'amuser *Tomorrow I shall be* (in the course of) *enjoying myself*

FOR REFERENCE: ORTHOGRAPHIC CHANGES IN GROUP I (-er)

1. Verbs with stem vowel in e-mute change this to è when the e becomes stressed or is followed by a mute syllable:

> **acheter** *to buy*: **j'achète, j'achèterai**
> **peser** *to weigh*: **je pèse, je pèserai**

Verbs with stem vowel in é change this to è when this is stressed:

protéger *to protect*: **je protège, il protège**, but **nous protégeons, vous protégez** and **ils protègent**

2. Verbs ending in **-cer, -ger** retain the soft **c** and soft **g** sounds in inflexions by changing **c** to **ç** and retaining the **ge** of the infinitive throughout before **a, o, u**. Thus:

> **commencer** *to begin*: **je commence**, but **nous commençons**
> **manger** *to eat*: **je mange**, but **nous mangeons**

This also occurs in other verbs:

> **recevoir** *to receive* **je reçois, j'ai reçu**

3. Verbs in **-eler** and **-eter** double the **l** or **t** when, in inflexion, the **l** or **t** follows the e-mute of the infinitive. Thus:

> **appeler** *to call*: **j'appelle, j'appellerai**
> **jeter** *to throw*: **je jette, je jetterai**

4. Verbs in **-ayer, oyer** and **-uyer** generally retain the **y** of the infinitive only when the vowel following it in inflexion is sounded:

> **balayer** *to sweep*: **je balaie**, but **nous balayons**
> **nettoyer** *to clean*: **je nettoie**, but **nous nettoyons**
> **essuyer** *to wipe*: **j'essuie**, but **nous essuyons**

However, the form *je balaye* may also be found sometimes.

Note: These orthographic changes are indicated in the Vocabulary at the end of the book with the letters OC + one of the above numbers to indicate the kind of change. Thus:

> **acheter** vtr (I, OC1) *to buy*
> **jeter** vtr (I, OC3) *to throw*

AFFIRMATIVE, INTERROGATIVE AND NEGATIVE FORMS

1. The affirmative: follows the same form as in English:

je parle *I speak, am speaking.* **vous finissez** *you finish, are finishing*

2. Interrogative: (*a*) the simplest interrogative form is made by using

the phrase **est-ce que . . . ?** *is it that . . . ?* (see p. 43) before the affirmative form:

> **Est-ce que je parle?** *Is it that I speak* = *Am I speaking?*

(*b*) by reversing the affirmative and putting the verb first and the personal pronoun after the verb:

> Simple tense: **Parlez-vous français?** *Do you speak French?*
> Compound tense: **Avez-vous fini?** *Have you finished?*

3. Negative forms: Negation is expressed by putting **ne** before the verb and **pas** after it:

Simple tense: **je ne donne pas** *I am not giving*
Compound tense: **je n'ai pas donné** *I did not give* (**ne** before aux, **pas**
                                                                                   after aux)

Similarly:

ne + verb $\left\{ \begin{array}{l} \text{+ \textbf{jamais} } \textit{never}\text{: \textbf{je ne donne jamais} } \textit{I never give} \\ \text{+ \textbf{plus} } \textit{no more, no longer}\text{: \textbf{je ne donne plus} } \textit{I no longer give} \\ \text{+ \textbf{rien} } \textit{nothing}\text{: \textbf{je n'ai rien} } \textit{I have nothing} \\ \text{+ \textbf{personne} } \textit{nobody}\text{: \textbf{il n'y a personne} } \textit{There is nobody, no one} \\ \text{+ \textbf{que} } \textit{only}\text{: \textbf{elle ne voit que la lune} } \textit{she only sees the moon} \end{array} \right.$

Before infinitives **ne** + second part of negative + verb:

> **ne pas parler** *not to speak*
> **ne jamais finir** *never to finish*

REFLEXIVE VERBS: MODEL CONJUGATION

A reflexive verb uses a reflexive personal pronoun (see column 4, Table, p. 32) to show that the action is both performed and suffered by the subject. Example: **se laver** *to wash oneself*.

je me lave	**je me laverai**	**je me suis lavé**
I wash myself, am washing myself	*I shall wash myself*	*I have washed myself*
tu te laves	**tu te laveras**	**tu t'es lavé**
il, elle se lave	**il, elle se lavera**	**il, elle, s'est lavé, -ée**
nous nous lavons	**nous nous laverons**	**nous nous sommes lavés**
vous vous lavez	**vous vous laverez**	**vous vous êtes lavés**
ils, elles se lavent	**ils, elles se laveront**	**ils se sont lavés**
		elles se sont lavées

Negative	Imperative	Interrogative
je ne me lave pas	lave-toi, lavons-nous	est-ce que je me lave?
tu ne te laves pas, etc.	lavez-vous	or, te laves-tu?, etc.

negative imperative:
ne te lave pas
ne nous lavons pas
ne vous lavez pas

se laver expresses true reflexive action. But in many French verbs the reflexive idea may be absent, to the foreign mind, as in: **se fâcher** *to be angry*; **se rappeler** *to recollect, remember*; and many others. All reflexive verbs are conjugated with **être**.

THE PASSIVE OF VERBS

This is formed in three ways, of which the first is the simplest.

1. By using **on** + object pronoun + verb: **on me lave** *(some-)one is washing me*. **On m'a lavé** *(some-)one washed me*, etc.

2. The reflexive form is often used in general statements:

le sucre et le sel se vendent chez l'épicier *sugar and salt are sold at the grocer's*

3. By using the required form of **être** + past participle of the main verb: **être aimé** *to be loved*. **il est aimé** *he is loved*. **elle est aimée** *she is loved*. **ils sont aimés** *they are loved*. See p. 50 for agreement of past participle.

IMPERSONAL VERBS

falloir (irregular Group III verb) is always used impersonally with one of these meanings: 1. to denote the need of something, 2. to denote an obligation or necessity. Like all truly impersonal verbs, it is used only in the 3rd pers sing.

Pres: **il faut.** Past: **il a fallu.** Fut: **il faudra**

Examples of 1:

il me faut cent francs *I need 100 francs*
il faut un jour pour aller à Paris *it needs (takes) a day to go to Paris*

Examples of 2:

> **il faut s'en aller** *one must go away from here*
> **il faut partir** *I, we, one must leave, go*

devoir can often be used instead of 2:

je dois m'en aller *I must go out, away*   **nous devons partir** *we must leave*

pleuvoir (irr Group III) *to rain*:

il pleut *it is raining*   **il a plu** *it rained, has rained*   **il pleuvra** *it will rain*

aller *to go* is often used to make the future of verbs, especially those dealing with weather:

> **il va neiger** *it is going to snow*
> **il va pleuvoir** *it is going to rain*
> **elle va arriver** *she is going to arrive*

y avoir there to be:

> **il y a** *there is, are*
> **il y a eu** *there was, were*
> **il y aura** *there will be*

Interrogative: **y a-t-il?** *is there?*   **y a-t-il eu?** *was there, were there?*   **y aura-t-il?** *will there be?*

Negative: **il n'y a pas, il n'y a pas eu, il n'y aura pas**

Some other French verbs can be used impersonally: **il paraît** *it seems*, etc.

avoir *to have* USED FOR ENGLISH *to be*

avoir
- **+ froid** *to be cold*: **j'ai froid** *I am cold*
- **+ chaud** *to be hot*
- **+ faim** *to be hungry*
- **+ soif** *to be thirsty*
- **+ raison** *to be right*
- **+ tort** *to be wrong*
- **+ sommeil** *to be sleepy*
- **+ peur** (de) *to be afraid (of)*
- **+ honte** (de) *to be ashamed (of)*
- **+ envie de** *to want to, to fancy, to be inclined to*
- **+ mal** (à *in*) *to have a pain (in)* = *to be sick (in)*
- **+ besoin** (de) *to need, lack* = *to be in want of*

THE FRENCH SUBJUNCTIVE

The French subjunctive tends to fall into disuse in everyday speech except in the present tense, and is now found mostly in written French. The tense-endings are given on p. 48.

Briefly, the subjunctive mood in French is used in a subordinate clause after verbs expressing doubt, desire, fear, surprise and will. One should be able to recognize it:

> **je doute qu'il vienne** *I doubt whether he will come*
> **il faut que je lui parle** *I must speak to him*
> **vous avez voulu qu'il parlât** *you wished that he should speak* (= *you wished for him to speak at that moment*)

It follows **avant que** *before* (*that*); **afin que** *in order that*; **de peur que** *for fear that*, and after some other such conjunctions as **quoique** *although* (see p. 67).

Note that **si** *if* is usually followed by the indicative although it may express doubt:

> **si c'est le même** *if it is* (*or be*) *the same*
> **s'il venait** *if he were to come*

venait is imperfect indicative (for endings see p. 48)

Avoiding the subjunctive: in speaking French the subjunctive can be avoided in simple statements:

> with subjunctive: **il faut que j'aille** (subj) *I must go*
> subj avoided in: **il faut aller** ⎱ *I must go*
> **je dois aller** ⎰

The subjunctive is found in some fairly common expressions such as **Dieu soit loué!** *May God be praised!* **Ainsi soit-il!** *So be it!*

PARTS OF VERBS USED AS OTHER PARTS OF SPEECH

The infinitive is often used as a noun:

> **le boire** *drinking* **le sourire** *smile, smiling*

Present participle: can sometimes be used as a noun:

> **un passant** *a passer-by*
> **les vivants** *the living* (*persons*)

Or as an adjective:

> **charmant, -e** *charming*
> **une femme charmante** *a charming woman*

Past participle: most past participles can be used as adjectives:

> **connu, -e** adj (from **connaître** *to know*) *known*
> **marié, -e** adj (from **marier** *to marry*) *married*

Parts of verbs used as other parts of speech follow the rules of those other parts of speech. See also Word building, p. 69.

MODELS FOR CONJUGATION OF REGULAR VERBS IN -er AND -ir

For classification, see p. 46.

Group I   Infinitives in -er

Every verb ending in **-er** except **aller** and **envoyer** is conjugated like **parler**.

parler *to speak*

Present participle **parlant** *speaking*.   Past participle **parlé** *spoken*

Present	Compound past	Future
je parle *I speak, am speaking, do speak*	**j'ai parlé** *I spoke, have spoken*	**je parlerai** *I shall speak*
tu parles	**tu as parlé**	**tu parleras**
il parle	**il a parlé**	**il parlera**
nous parlons	**nous avons parlé**	**nous parlerons**
vous parlez	**vous avez parlé**	**vous parlerez**
ils parlent	**ils ont parlé**	**ils parleront**

Imperative
parle *speak* (*you* fam)
parlons *let us speak*
parlez *speak* (*you* s & pl)

Group II

Infinitives in **-ir** and taking in **-iss-** in the present participle. These are 'regular'. All other **-ir** verbs are Group III and 'irregular', see pp. 47.

finir *to finish*

Present participle **finissant** *finishing*. Past participle **fini** *finished*

Present	Compound past	Future
je finis *I finish, am finishing*	**j'ai fini** *I finished, have finished*	**je finirai** *I shall finish*
tu finis	**tu as fini**	**tu finiras**
il finit	**il a fini**	**il finira**
nous finissons	**nous avons fini**	**nous finirons**
vous finissez	**vous avez fini**	**vous finirez**
ils finissent	**ils ont fini**	**ils finiront**

Imperative

finis *finish* (*you* fam)
finissons *let us finish*
finissez *finish* (*you* s & pl)

For agreement of past participles, see p. 50.

Group III   Irregular verbs

The number of these required for most everyday purposes has been reduced to about 50 in this book (out of some hundreds of irregular French verbs!). The 'basic' parts of the essential Group III verbs are given in the pages that follow.

Verbs conjugated with **être** are marked with asterisk *.

Present participles indicate the stem and are placed after other parts, to the right of the page.

1. ending -er

*__aller__ *to go*

Pres: **je vais, tu vas, il va, nous allons, vous allez, ils vont**. Pa: **je suis allé**. Fut: **j'irai, -as, -a, -ons, -ez, -ont**. Pa part: **allé**   (allant)

envoyer *to send*

Pres: **j'envoie, nous envoyons**. Irr fut: **j'enverrai, tu enverras,** etc.

(Takes **i** instead of **y** before **e**-mute.)

Pa part: **envoyé**   (envoyant)

58 — *The Basis of Grammar*

2. ending **-ir**

For **-ir** verbs which take in **-ss-**, see pp. 56 and Group II, p. 47. Those which do not take in **-ss-** are irr and therefore listed below:

dormir *to sleep*

Pres: je dors, tu dors, il dort, nous dormons, vous dormez, ils dorment.
Pa: j'ai dormi. Fut: je dormirai, etc. Pa part: dormi   (dormant)

*partir *to leave*

Pres: je pars, tu pars, il part, nous partons, -ez, -ent. Pa: je suis parti.
Fut: je partirai. Pa part: parti   (partant)

sentir vtr *to feel*

Pres: je sens, tu sens, il sent, nous sentons, -ez, -ent. Pa: j'ai senti. Fut:
je sentirai, etc. Pa part: senti   (sentant)
se sentir (bien, mal, gai) vintr *to feel (well, faint, gay)*

*sortir *to go out*

Pres: je sors, tu sors, il sort, nous sortons, -ez, -ent. Pa: je suis sorti. Fut:
je sortirai. Pa part: sorti   (sortant)

servir *to serve*

Pres: je sers, tu sers, il sert, nous servons, -ez, -ent. Pa: j'ai servi. Fut: je
servirai. Pa part: servi   (servant)
se servir *to help oneself.* se servir de *to make use of*

*mourir *to die*

Pres: je meurs, tu meurs, il meurt, nous mourons, -ez, ils meurent. Pa: je
suis mort. Fut: je mourrai. Pa part: mort   (mourant)

tenir *to hold*

Pres: je tiens, tu tiens, il tient, nous tenons, -ez, ils tiennent. Pa: j'ai
tenu. Fut: je tiendrai. Pa part: tenu   (tenant)

Similarly: **obtenir** *to obtain*

*venir *to come*

Pres: je viens, tu viens, il vient, nous venons, -ez, ils viennent. Pa: je suis
venu. Fut: je viendrai. Pa part: venu   (venant)

couvrir *to cover*

Pres: je couvre, tu couvres, il couvre, nous couvrons, -ez, -ent. Pa: j'ai
couvert. Fut: je couvrirai. Pa part: couvert   (couvrant)

ouvrir *to open*

>Pres: j'ouvre, tu ouvres, il ouvre, nous ouvrons, -ez, -ent. Pa: j'ai ouvert.
>Fut: j'ouvrirai. Pa part: ouvert .... (ouvrant)

cueillir *to gather, to pluck*

>Pres: je cueille, tu cueilles, il cueille, nous cueillons, -ez, -ent. Pa: j'ai
>cueilli. Fut: je cueillerai. Pa part: cueilli .... (cueillant)

courir *to run*

>Pres: je cours, tu cours, il court, nous courons, -ez, -ent. Pa: j'ai couru.
>Fut: je courrai. Pa part: couru .... (courant)

>Similarly: **concourir** *to compete.* **parcourir** *to travel through.*
>   **secourir** *to help.* **accourir** *to hasten to.*

vêtir tr *to clothe*

>Pres: je vêts, tu vêts, il vêt, nous vêtons, -ez, -ent. Pa: j'ai vêtu. Fut: je
>vêtirai. Pa part: vêtu .... (vêtant)
>se vêtir *to dress oneself* (more usual form)

3. ending -oir

avoir aux, see p. 48.

devoir *to have to, to owe*

>Pres: je dois, tu dois, il doit, nous devons, -ez, ils doivent. Pa: j'ai dû.
>Fut: je devrai. Pa part: dû .... (devant)

recevoir *to receive*

>Pres: je reçois, tu reçois, il reçoit, nous recevons, -ez, ils reçoivent. Pa:
>j'ai reçu. Fut: je recevrai. Pa part: reçu .... (recevant)

pouvoir *to be able to*

>Pres: je peux, tu peux, il peut (also je puis), nous pouvons, -ez, ils peuvent.
>Pa: j'ai pu. Fut: je pourrai. Pa part: pu .... (pouvant)

vouloir *to wish, to want*

>Pres: je veux, tu veux, il veut, nous voulons, -ez, ils veulent. Pa: j'ai voulu.
>Fut: je voudrai. Pa part: voulu .... (voulant)

savoir *to know*

>Pres: je sais, tu sais, il sait, nous savons, -ez, -ent. Pa: j'ai su. Fut:
>je saurai. Pa part: su .... (sachant)
>Never used for to know a person, but of knowledge from education,
>training, practice or skill. See **connaître**.
>savoir + inf *to know how to*

5—B.E.F.

voir *to see*

> Pres: je vois, tu vois, il voit, nous voyons, -ez, ils voient. Pa: j'ai vu. Fut:
> je verrai. Pa part: vu   (voyant)

*s'asseoir *to sit down*

> Pres: je m'assieds, tu t'assieds, il s'assied, nous nous asseyons, vous vous
> asseyez, ils s'asseyent. Pa: je me suis assis. Fut: je m'assiérai. Pa part:
> assis   (s'asseyant)
> Another form: Pres: je m'assois, nous nous assoyons. Fut: je m'assoirai.
> Pa part: assis   (s'assoyant)
> Use the first form, be able to recognize the second.

falloir
pleuvoir } Impersonal verbs, see p. 53.

4. ending in **-re**

être aux, see p. 48.

boire *to drink*

> Pres: je bois, tu bois, il boit, nous buvons, vous buvez, ils boivent. Pa: j'ai
> bu. Fut: je boirai. Pa part: bu   (buvant)

croire *to believe*

> Pres: je crois, tu crois, il croit, nous croyons, -ez, ils croient. Pa: j'ai cru.
> Fut: je croirai. Pa part: cru   (croyant)

*descendre *to go* (or *to come*) *down*

> Pres: je descends, tu descends, il descend, nous descendons, -ez, -ent. Pa:
> je suis descendu. Fut: je descendrai. Pa part: descendu   (descendant)

entendre *to hear, to listen, to understand*

> Pres: j'entends, tu entends, il entend, nous entendons, -ez, -ent. Pa: j'ai
> entendu. Fut: j'entendrai. Pa part: entendu   (entendant)

coudre *to sew*

> Pres: je couds, tu couds, il coud, nous cousons, vous cousez, ils cousent.
> Pa: j'ai cousu. Fut: je coudrai. Pa part: cousu   (cousant)

mordre *to bite*

> Pres: je mords, tu mords, il mord, nous mordons, -ez, -ent. Pa: j'ai mordu.
> Fut: je mordrai. Pa part: mordu   (mordant)

répondre *to reply*

> Pres: je réponds, tu réponds, il répond, nous répondons, -ez, -ent. Pa: j'ai
> répondu. Fut: je répondrai. Pa part: répondu   (répondant)

vendre *to sell*

>Pres: je vends, tu vends, il vend, nous vendons, -ez, -ent. Pa: j'ai vendu.
>Fut: je vendrai. Pa part: vendu   (vendant)

prendre *to take*

>Pres: je prends, tu prends, il prend, nous prenons, -ez, ils prennent. Pa:
>j'ai pris. Fut: je prendrai. Pa part: pris   (prenant)

mettre *to put*

>Pres: je mets, tu mets, il met, nous mettons, -ttez, -ttent. Pa: j'ai mis.
>Fut: je mettrai. Pa part: mis   (mettant)

suivre *to follow*

>Pres: je suis, tu suis, il suit, nous suivons, -ez, -ent. Pa: j'ai suivi. Fut: je
>suivrai. Pa part: suivi   (suivant)

vivre *to live*

>Pres: je vis, tu vis, il vit, nous vivons, -ez, -ent. Pa: j'ai vécu. Fut: je
>vivrai. Pa part: vécu   (vivant)

lire *to read*

>Pres: je lis, tu lis, il lit, nous lisons, -ez, -ent. Pa: j'ai lu. Fut: je lirai. Pa
>part: lu   (lisant)

écrire *to write*

>Pres: j'écris, tu écris, il écrit, nous écrivons, -ez, -ent. Pa: j'ai écrit. Fut:
>j'écrirai. Pa part: écrit   (écrivant)

conduire *to lead, to drive, to guide*

>Pres: je conduis, tu conduis, il conduit, nous conduisons, -ez, -ent. Pa: j'ai
>conduit. Fut: je conduirai. Pa part: conduit   (conduisant)

dire *to say, to tell*

>Pres: je dis, tu dis, il dit, nous disons, vous dites, ils disent. Pa: j'ai dit.
>Fut: je dirai. Pa part: dit   (disant)

plaire *to please*

>Pres: je plais, tu plais, il plaît, nous plaisons, -ez, -ent. Pa: j'ai plu. Fut:
>je plairai. Pa part: plu   (plaisant)

se taire *to be silent*

>Pres: je me tais, tu te tais, il se tait, nous nous taisons, vous vous taisez,
>ils se taisent. Pa: je me suis tu. Fut: je me tairai. Pa part: tu (se taisant)

connaître *to be acquainted with, to know*

Pres: je connais, tu connais, il connaît, nous connaissons, vous connaissez, ils connaissent. Pa: j'ai connu. Fut: je connaîtrai. Pa part: connu
(connaissant)

Meaning of **connaître**: to be acquainted with a person, to have a general knowledge of something. (Compare with **savoir**.)

*naître *to be born*

Pres: je nais, tu nais, il naît, nous naissons, -ez, -ent. Pa (commonest form): je suis né (née). Fut: je naîtrai. Pa part: né   (naissant)

paraître *to appear*

Pres: je parais, tu parais, il paraît, nous paraissons, -ez, -ent. Pa: j'ai paru. Fut: je paraîtrai. Pa part: paru   (paraissant)

faire *to make, to do*

Pres: je fais, tu fais, il fait, nous faisons, vous faites, ils font. Pa: j'ai fait. Fut: je ferai. Pa part: fait   (faisant)
(See notes on **faire** below.)

rire *to laugh*

Pres: je ris, tu ris, il rit, nous rions, vous riez, ils rient. Pa: j'ai ri. Fut: je rirai. Pa part: ri   (riant)

peindre *to paint*

Pres: je peins, tu peins, il peint, nous peignons, vous peignez, ils peignent. Pa: j'ai peint. Fut: je peindrai. Pa part: peint   (peignant)

Similarly: **éteindre** *to put out, to extinguish.* **teindre** *to dye.*

See p. 55 for parts of verbs used as other parts of speech.

| aller | s'en aller | faire |

Basic meanings: *to go   to go out, away, off   (1) to make (2) to do*

These verbs will require more attention than can be given to them in a book of this nature, because of the wide range of uses and the many idiomatic expressions into which they may enter. The following examples give some idea of this:

aller:

Allez! *Go on, go ahead*
aller à pied *to go on foot, to walk*
aller chercher *to go and get = to fetch*
Les affaires vont bien *Business is brisk*
Les affaires ne vont pas *Business is slack*

Comment allez-vous? *How are you?*
aller + inf *to be going to do something*
Je vais fumer *I am going to have a smoke*
J'y vais or **On y va** *Coming!*
aller se promener *to go for a walk, a stroll*
Allons! *Come now!*
Allons donc! *Nonsense!*
un billet d'aller et retour *a return ticket*

s'en aller:

Je m'en vais *I'm off*
Allez-vous-en! *Go away!*
Le malade s'en va *The patient is sinking*

faire:

se faire des amis *to make friends*
Que faire? *What is to be done?*
Il n'y a rien à faire *There's nothing to be done about it*
avoir de quoi faire *to have one's work cut out*
Faites donc! *By all means (do so)*
Faites vite! *Be quick*
On m'a fait *I've been done, had*

faire + inf is causative:

faire faire quelque chose *to get (cause) something (to be) done*
faire bâtir une maison *to get a house built*
faire coucher un enfant *to put a child to bed*

faire impers:

il fait beau (temps) *it's fine (weather)*
il fait du soleil *it is sunny*
il fait mauvais voyager par ces routes *it is hard going on these roads*

INVARIABLE WORDS

ADVERBS

There are two kinds of adverbs in French:

1. those which by their nature are adverbs and do not derive from any other word. Examples: **très** *very*, **plus** *more*, **où** *where*, **ici** *here*, **là** *there*, **bientôt** *soon*, **encore** *still, yet*. These will be found in dictionaries and in the Vocabulary at the end.

2. those which are made from or of other words, like **heureusement**, made from the feminine form of the adjective **heureux** *happy*. These are the majority of French adverbs and correspond to English adverbs ending in *-ly*: *courageous* (adj), *courageously* (adv).

General rule for formation: Add **-ment** to the feminine form of the adjective. Thus:

heureux, heureuse, adv **heureusement   doux, douce** *soft* **doucement**
sec, sèche *dry* **sèchement**

Adjectives ending in **-ant, -ent,** drop **-ant** or **-ent** and substitute **-amment,-emment**. Thus:

obligeant *obliging* **obligeamment**

Except: **lent** *slow* **lentement**

Adjectives ending in **é, -i, -u, -ai,** simply add **-ment**:

assuré *sure, firm* **assurément   vrai** *true* **vraiment**

Irregularities: Note **bref, brièvement.   gentil, gentiment.**

Adverbial expressions of time:

d'aujourd'hui en huit *this day week* (future)
il y a quinze jours aujourd'hui *a fortnight ago*
il y a dix ans *ten years ago*

avant-hier *the day before yesterday*   **hier** *yesterday*   **aujourd'hui** *today*
demain *tomorrow*   **après-demain** *the day after tomorrow*

Comparison of adverbs

Like that of adjectives:

> adj **rapide**, adv **rapidement**
> > **plus rapidement que** ... *more quickly than* ...
> Superlative   **le plus rapidement** *most quickly*

Irregularities:

adv **mal** *badly*	**plus mal** or **pis** *worse*	**le plus mal** or **le pis** *worst*
bien *well*	**mieux** *better*	**le mieux** *best*
adj **petit** *small*	**moins** *less*	**le moins** *least*
adv **peu** *little*		

> **Jean parle mieux que Charles** *John speaks better than Charles*

Constructions to note: *more than* before a number = **plus de**:

> **Je travaille plus de cinq heures par jour** *I work more than five hours a day*

After superlative **de** = *in*:

> **le plus belle maison de Londres** *the nicest house in London*

It is better to **il vaut mieux** + inf:

> **il vaut mieux parler à Marie** *better speak to Mary*

davantage adv *more, longer, still more, still longer* (usually at the end of a statement):

> **ne pas en dire davantage** *to say no more about it*
> **bien davantage** *much more*

PREPOSITIONS

The basic prepositions in French are:

à (1) *at, in, to, by, on*
à cause (de) *because (of)*
à côté (de) *beside, near, close to*
à droite (de) *to the right (of)*
à gauche (de) *to the left (of)*
après *after*
au bout (de) *at the end (of)*
au-dessous (de) *below*
au-dessus (de) *above, on*

au milieu (de) *in the middle (of)*
autour (de) *around, about*
avant *before*
avec *with*
chez *at the home (house) of*
contre *against*
dans (4) *in, among, into, within*
de (2) *of, from, about, out of, by, for*

depuis *since, from, for* (*time*)
derrière *behind*
devant *in front of, before*
en (3) *in, to, into, at, on, of, from*
en dehors (de) *outside of, beyond, apart from*
en face (de) *across from, opposite*
entre *between, among*
jusque, jusqu'(à) *until* (*time*), *as far as* (space)

loin (de) *far* (*from*)
par *by, on, through, out of, in, per*
pendant *during*
pour *in order to* (+verb)
près (de) *near, close* (*to*)
sans *without, free of* (or *from*)
sous *under, below, beneath*
sur *on, in*
vers *towards, about* (time, number)

(1), (2), (3), (4) are the most troublesome, see below. The others are mostly straightforward.

1. à: *at, in* (towns, not countries): **à Londres** *in London*
     to (movement): **je vais à Paris** *I am going to Paris*
     from (distance):
          j'habite à 20 kilomètres d'ici *I live* (*at*) *20 km from here*
     by (manner): **fait à la main** *made by hand*   **à pied** *on foot*
                    à la livre *by the pound* (*lb*)
     at (time): **à midi, minuit** *at noon, midnight*
          à dix heures *at ten o'clock*
     for (purpose): **une tasse à thé** *a teacup*

2. de: *of* (content): **une tasse de thé** *a cup of tea*
     of, made of: **une table de bois** *a wooden table*
     from (direction): **je viens de Paris** *I come from Paris*
     of (possession, ownership):
          la maison de mon oncle *my uncle's house*

3. en: *in, into* (not followed by article): **en France** *in France*
          en Espagne *in Spain* (en not used for towns)
     of (state of): **en guerre** *at war* (*in a state of war*)
          en hiver *in winter*. But: **au printemps** *in spring*
     of, made of (substance): **en or** (*made*) *of gold*

4. dans: *in* (place, no movement):
               il est dans son bureau *he is in his office*
               dans la rue *in the street*
          in, into (place, movement):
               je l'ai mis dans le tiroir *I put it into the drawer*
               je marche dans la rue *I am walking in the street*

CONJUNCTIONS

The basic conjunctions are:

*avant que *before	parce que *because*
depuis que *since*	pendant que *while*
donc *so, therefore*	*pour que *so that*
mais *but*	quand *while, at the time when*
et *and*	que, qu' *that, than, till*
ni ... ni ... *neither ... nor ...*	que (after comparative) *than*
ou *or*	quoique, quoiqu' *although*
	si (conditional) *if, whether*

* The subjunctive is used after these conjunctions. This can usually be avoided by using (*1*) **avant de**+infinitive:

> **je me lave avant de sortir** *I wash before going out*

instead of:

> **je me lave avant que je sorte** (subj)

and (*2*) **pour**+infinitive:

j'attends ma mère pour sortir avec elle *I am waiting for my mother to go out with her*

instead of:

> **j'attends ma mère pour que je sorte** (subj) **avec elle**

EXCLAMATORY WORDS AND PHRASES

Allons! *Come now!*	**Comment donc?** *What is that?*
Allons donc! *Go on!*	**Comment donc!** *How* (= *why*) *is that!* (expresses surprise)
Assez! *Enough!*	
Bien! *Fine! O.K.*	**Gare!** *Look out!* (danger)
Bien sûr! *Why certainly! Of course!*	**Pas possible!** *Impossible!*
	Tiens! *Well!*
Très bien! *Very good! Spendid!*	**Voyons!** *Come, come!*
Bis! *Again! Encore!*	**Vrai!** *Really!* (surprise)
Bon! *Good!*	**Vraiment!** *Is that so?*
Très bon! *Excellent! Fine!*	**Zut!** *Bother!*
Comment! *What!*	

Que *how,* **combien** *how much, many,* used to make many exclamatory phrases:

> **Que je suis content!** *How pleased I am!*
> **Combien de bouteilles!** *What a lot of bottles!*
> **Que faire?** *What is to be done?*
> **Que penser?** *What is one to think?*

And the imperative of any verb:

> **Arrêtons-nous!** *Let us stop!*
> **Allons!** *Come on! Let's go!*

WORD BUILDING

For the purpose here, French has four practical ways of making new or compound words from simple ones:

1. by adding a prefix: **faire** *to do*. **refaire** *to redo, do again*
2. by adding a suffix: **la raison** *reason*. **raisonner** *to reason*.

All new verbs added to the language today end in **-er** and belong to Group 1.

3. by joining two existing words: **aigre** *sour* + **doux** *sweet* **aigre-doux** *bitter-sweet, subacid*
4. by using one part of speech for another:

boire vtr *to drink*. **le boire** n *drinking*. **froid** adj *cold*. **le froid** (*the*) *cold* n

Prefixes used in word building

dé- reverse meaning of basic word: **couvrir** *to cover*. **découvrir** *to uncover* also *to discover*

contre- action against: **dire** *to say*. **contredire** *to contradict*

im-		**possible** *possible*	**impossible** *impossible*
il-	negation:	**lisible** *legible*	**illisible** *illegible*
ir-		**religieux** *religious*	**irreligieux** *irreligious*
in-		**sensible** *sensitive*	**insensible** *insensitive*

mi- *half, mid-*: **août** *August*. **la mi-août** *mid-August*
clos adj *closed*. **mi-clos** *half-closed*

re-
r(é)- *again*: **lire** *to read*. **relire** *to re-read*
établir *to establish*. **rétablir** *to re-establish, restore*

sou(s)-
sub- *under*: **lever** *to raise*. **soulever** *to lift up* (from underneath)
diviser *to divide*. **subdiviser** *to subdivide*

sur- *over*: **voler** *to fly*. **survoler** *to fly over*

Suffixes used in word building

To form nouns:

-age act of: **laver** *to wash.* **le lavage** *washing*

-ier occupation: **la ferme** *farm.* **le fermier** *farmer*
-ière   **la fermière** *woman farmer,* also *farmer's wife*

-ée f collective, ⎱ **la feuille** *leaf.* **la feuillée** *foliage*
   contents: ⎰ **la bouche** *mouth.* **la bouchée** *mouthful*

-eur m ⎱ doer,   **voyager** *to travel.* **le voyageur** *traveller, passenger*
-euse f ⎰ agent: **blanchir** *to whiten, wash.* **la blanchisseuse** *laundress*

-ion ⎱ mostly   **illuminer** *to light up.* **l'illumination** *floodlighting*
-tion ⎰ abstract ns **importer** *to import.* **l'importation** *import*
-sion ⎰ (all fem): **immerger** *to immerse.* **une immersion** *immersion,*
                                                              plunge

-té (abstractness): **léger, légère** adj *light.* **la légèreté** *lightness*
      (all fem)

-iste *-ist* ⎱ social adj *social* ⎰ **socialiste** *socialist*
-isme *-ism* ⎰   ⎰ **socialisme** *socialism*

   Adjectival suffixes:

-able ⎱ quality of: **durer** *to last.* **durable** *lasting, durable*
-ible ⎰   **la paix** *peace.* **paisible** *peaceful*

-ais ⎱ common among adjs **la France.** **français** *French*
-ois ⎰ of nationality: **la Hongrie.** **hongrois** *Hungarian*
        ⎰ see pp. 80–1

-é ⎱ pa parts as adjs: **soigner** *to care, look after*
-ée ⎰   **soigné(e)** *cared for, groomed, spruce*

   Adverbial suffix **-ment** *-ly*:

            solide *solid.* **solidement** *solidly* (p. 64)

   Verbal suffix **-er** to form new verbs:

le téléphone *telephone* **téléphoner** *to telephone*
la télévision *television* **téléviser** *to televise* **téléviseur** *television set*

Note: Some of the above words, not being essential, are omitted
from the vocabulary at the end of the book.

IDIOMS

An idiom is a form of expression peculiar to a language. Alternatively, it is a group of words of which the meaning is not clear from their primary sense. Thus: **Vous l'avez échappé belle** is a French idiom meaning literally, *You have escaped from it beautifully*, or, *You've had a narrow escape* (or, *You've had a narrow squeak*, or, *It's been a narrow squeak for you*). And **être de trop**, literally *to be (one) too many = to be unwelcome* or *in the way*.

French idioms are best learnt by experience rather than by memorizing lists: the circumstances in which an idiom is used often determine its meaning. The following are in everyday use:

Que voulez-vous dire? *What do you mean?*   **vouloir dire** *to mean*

Qu'est-ce qu'il y a? *What is the matter?*

De quoi s'agit-il? *What's it about?*

Qu'est-ce qu'il a?
Qu'est-ce qu'elle a? } *What is the matter with him/her?*

Il n'y a pas de quoi *Don't mention it*

S'il vous plaît *If you please, please*

Plaît-il? *I beg your pardon? What did you say?*

Quel temps fait-il? *What (or How) is the weather?*

Il fait beau temps *The weather is fine*

Il fait beau, froid, etc. *It is hot, cold,* etc.

Avoir mal à *to have a pain in*

    J'ai mal au cœur *I feel sick*

    J'ai mal aux dents *I have a toothache*

Me voici! *Here I am!*

Vous voilà! *There you are!*

Le combien sommes-nous? *What is the date?*

Nous sommes le ... *The date is ...*

Il me faut
Il vous faut } (a) + infinitive *I must, you must, he must,* etc.
Il lui faut, etc. } (b) + noun *I want, need,* etc.
        from **falloir**, see p. 53.

Tout ce qu'il me faut *All that I need*

Vous devez + infinitive *You must.* **Vous devez y aller** *You must go there*

Veuillez+infinitive *Please . . .* or, *Be so kind as to . . .*

    Veuillez me suivre *Kindly follow me*

Merci *Thanks, thank you,* and also *no thanks, no thank you*

Prenez-vous du café? *Do you take, will you take coffee?*

    Answer: **Merci** *No, thank you* or *Yes please* (depending
                on the tone of voice)

          S'il vous plaît *Yes, please*

Merci bien *Thank you very much*

Je vous remercie (bien) more formal *Thank you (very much)*

Je vous en prie *That's all right, please do*

acheter à bon marché *to buy cheap(ly)*

acheter à crédit *to buy on credit, on H.P.*

acheter d'occasion *to buy second-hand*

payer à boire *to stand a drink*

boire un coup *to have a drink*

boire sec *to drink neat*

manger à sa faim *to eat one's fill*

manger comme quatre *to make a huge meal, eat like a horse*

manger son argent *to squander one's money*

manger le chemin *to devour the way* (= *to eat up the miles*)

dormir profondément *to be sound asleep*

faire la grasse matinée *to have a lie-in*

See also: p. 62: **aller, s'en aller, faire**

LETTER WRITING

The date is written:

Le 1er janvier 1968. Le 31 décembre 1968

A formal opening:

Monsieur, Messieurs, Madame, Mesdames, Mademoiselle,

Mesdemoiselles. Text of letter follows.

A moderately familiar opening:

Cher Monsieur, Chère Madame, Mademoiselle,
or **Cher Monsieur X, etc.**

A familiar opening:

Mon cher Dupont, Mon cher Georges, Ma chère Hélène.

A formal ending:

Veuillez agréer, Monsieur, l'expression de mes sentiments distingués.

A moderately familiar ending:

Croyez en mes sentiments distingués.

A friendly ending:

Cordialement à vous.   Amicalement.

Familiar endings:

Tout à vous (= *yours ever*).   **Amitiés.**

METRIC SYSTEM AND APPROXIMATE EQUIVALENTS

LINEAR MEASURE

10 cm= **10 centimètres**=4 inches
30 centimètres=almost 1 foot
1 m=**1 mètre**=3 feet 3 inches
1 km=**1 kilomètre**=four-fifths of 1 mile
8 kilomètres=5 miles

WEIGHTS

1 g=**1 gramme**=0·03 of 1 ounce
28⅓ grammes=1 ounce
113 grammes=¼ lb
227 grammes=½ lb
454 grammes=1 lb avoirdupois
500 g=**1** (une) **livre** or **1 demi-kilo**
1 000 grammes=*1 kg*
1 kg=**1 kilo**=**1 kilogramme**=$2\frac{1}{10}$ lb avoirdupois
500 kilogrammes=9 cwt 3 qrs 11 lb
1 t=**1 tonne**=*1000 kg*=2,205 lb

Note: **kilogramme** is usually shortened to **kilo** and *kg* is pronounced **kilo.**

SQUARE MEASURE

1 m²=**1 mètre carré** (*sq. metre*)=1⅓ sq. yd.
0,91 m=1 yd.
0,836 mètre carré=1 sq. yd.
5 mètres carrés=6 sq. yd.
1 hectare=**10.000 mètres carrés**=nearly 2½ acres

FLUID MEASURE

1 l=**1 litre**=1·76 pints=about 1¾ pints
0,56 l=1 pint
4,54 l=1 gallon
1 décalitre=**10 litres**=$2\frac{1}{10}$ gallons
1 hectolitre=**100 litres**=22 gallons

THE THERMOMETER

5° centigrade=9° Fahrenheit=4° Réaumur

Freezing point:

Centigrade and Réaumur=0°
Fahrenheit=32°

Boiling point:

Centigrade=100°. Réaumur=80°
Fahrenheit=212°

Normal blood heat:

Centigrade=37°. Réaumur=29·8°
Fahrenheit=98·4°

Degrees centigrade multiplied by 1·8+32=degrees Fahrenheit.
Degrees Fahrenheit minus 32 multiplied by 0·55=degrees centigrade.

PART 2

THE ESSENTIAL VOCABULARY

VOCABULARY

The essential vocabulary of French, that is, a vocabulary with which one can act in most of the situations of everyday life, is given alphabetically in the pages that follow. In order to use this vocabulary effectively, one must know the elements or basis of grammar, given on pp. 14–70. The range of this material can be greatly extended with the use of common idioms, and phrases, some of which are used almost as frequently as the essential words. These are given with the words in the vocabulary. Look up the word **y**, for example, and you will see that the basic meanings of this word as an adv or prep are illustrated by ten quite common phrases and idioms. The French–English vocabulary given here consists of:

1. Essential French words and meanings.

2. Useful phrases and idioms to illustrate or extend their primary meanings.

Certain words should be learnt at an early stage: the numeral words on pp. 28–30, days of the week, months of the year, public holidays in France, and some geographical names as well as adjectives of nationality. These are given below for convenience of learning or reference:

DAYS OF THE WEEK LES JOURS DE LA SEMAINE

all m **lundi** *Monday*   **vendredi** *Friday*
       mardi *Tuesday*   **samedi** *Saturday*
       mercredi *Wednesday* **dimanche** *Sunday*
       jeudi *Thursday*

Note: Monday is considered to be the first day of the week.

MONTHS OF THE YEAR LES MOIS DE L'ANNÉE

janvier *January*   **mars** *March*
février *February*   **avril** *April*

mai *May*   septembre *September*
juin *June*   octobre *October*
juillet *July*   novembre *November*
août *August*   décembre *December*

SEASONS LES SAISONS

le printemps *spring*   un or une automne *autumn*
un été *summer*   un hiver *winter*

PUBLIC HOLIDAYS LES JOURS DE FÊTE

le jour de fête *Bank* or *public holiday, feast day, festival*
le or la Noël *Christmas*   Pâques fpl *Easter*
la Pentecôte *Whitsuntide*   la pâque *Jewish Passover*

GEOGRAPHICAL NAMES AND ADJECTIVES OF NATIONALITY

l'Allemagne nf *Germany*   allemand, -e *German*
l'Amérique nf *America*   américain, -e *American*
l'Angleterre nf *England*   anglais, -e *English*
l'Autriche nf *Austria*   autrichien, -ne *Austrian*
la Belgique *Belgium*   belge (m & f) *Belgian*
le Brésil *Brazil*   brésilien, -ne *Brazilian*
le Canada *Canada*   canadien, -ne *Canadian*
la Chine *China*   chinois, -e *Chinese*
l'Ecosse nf *Scotland*   écossais, -e *Scottish*
l'Espagne nf *Spain*   espagnol, -e *Spanish*
la Grande-Bretagne *Great Britain*   britannique (m & f) *British*
la Hollande (= les Pays-Bas)   hollandais, -e *Dutch*
     Holland
la Hongrie *Hungary*   hongrois, -e *Hungarian*
l'Inde, les Indes nf *India*   indien, -ne *Indian*
l'Irlande nf *Ireland*   irlandais, -e *Irish*
l'Italie nf *Italy*   italien, -ne *Italian*
le Japon *Japan*   japonais, -e *Japanese*
la Norvège *Norway*   norvégien, -ne *Norwegian*
la Pologne *Poland*   polonais, -e *Polish*
le Portugal *Portugal*   portugais, -e *Portuguese*

la Russie *Russia*	**russe** (m & f) *Russian*
la Suisse *Switzerland*	**suisse** (m & f) *Swiss*

l'URSS = l'Union des Républiques Socialistes Soviétiques
  USSR = Union of Soviet Socialist Republics

l'Afrique nf *Africa*	**africain, -e** *African*
l'Asie nf *Asia*	**asiatique** *Asian*
l'Australie nf *Australia*	**australien, -ne** *Australian*
l'Europe nf *Europe*	**européen, -ne** *European*

La Manche *the English Channel*
La Mer Méditerranée *the Mediterranean Sea*
La Mer du Nord *the North Sea*

Note: Capital letters are not used in French for days of the week, months, or adjectives (including adjectives of nationality). **Il est Anglais** has a capital because **Anglais** is used as a noun = *He is an Englishman = He is English.* However, **le français** *the French language* does not take a capital.

GENDER OF NOUNS AND CONJUGATION OF VERBS IN THE VOCABULARY

Gender of nouns

This is indicated by the definite article placed after each noun:
  bain, le n *bath.* **banque, la** n *bank* (finance house)
  When a noun begins with a vowel or h-mute, the indefinite article has been placed after it since the definite article would not make the gender clear because of elision. Thus:
  agent, un n *agent.* **affaire, une** n *business; matter*

Conjugation of verbs

All verbs are followed by an indication in brackets of their conjugation. Thus:

aimer (vtr) (I) *to love*	See pp. 46–8 for the three
mener (vtr) (I, OC) *to lead*	Groups of verbs marked
finir (vtr) (II, with -ss-) *to finish*	(I), (II), (III) in the
partir (vintr) (III) *to set out, to leave, to go*	vocabulary.
aller (vintr) (III) *to go*	The letters OC = orthographic changes for Group I verbs.
savoir (vintr) (III) *to know*	See p. 50
dire (vtr) (III) *to say*	

ESSENTIAL VOCABULARY

FRENCH/ENGLISH
(for abbreviations used, see p. viii)

A

à (prep) [time]
  à quatre heures *at 4 o'clock*
  à temps *in time*
à (prep) [place]
  à Paris, à Londres *in Paris, in London*
  Note: **à moi, à lui** *mine, his* (see p. 36)
d'abord (adv) *firstly, at first*
abbé, un (n) *abbot; parish priest* [R.C.]
accent, un (n) *accent* (` ´ ˆ); *pronunciation*
  parler français sans accent *to speak French without a (foreign) accent* = *to speak with a good pronunciation*
accident, un (n) *accident*
d'accord (adv) *in agreement*
  être d'accord *to agree*
  D'accord! *Agreed!*
acheter (vtr) (I, OC, 1) *to buy*
acte, un (n) 1. *act.* 2. *deed* [legal]
action, une (n) *action*
activité, une (n) *activity*
adresse, une (n) *address*
adroit, -e (adj) *skilful; handy*
affaire, une (n) *business; matter*
affaires, les (npl) *affairs, business, business matters*
  être dans les affaires *to be in business*

âge, un (n) *age; time of life*
  Quel âge avez-vous? *How old are you?*
  J'ai dix ans *I am ten*
agent, un (n) *agent*
agent (de police), un (n) *policeman*
agréable (adj) *pleasant; nice*
aider (vtr) (I) *to help*
aide, une (n) *help.* **un aide** *helper, assistant.* **aide-** + noun = *assistant* + noun. **un aide-infirmier** *assistant nurse* (m). **une aide-infirmière** *assistant nurse* (f)
aiguille, une (n) *needle*
  les aiguilles d'une montre *hands of a watch*
aile, une (n) *wing* [of bird, aeroplane]
aimer (vtr) (I) *to like, to love*
  Je l'aime *I love him, her*
  Je l'aime *bien I like him, her*
ainsi (adv) *thus; in this (that) manner*
air, l' (nm) *air*
ajouter (vtr) (I) *to add*
aller (vintr) (III) *to go* [with **être**]
  Comment allez-vous? *How are you?*
  Je vais bien, merci *I am well, thanks.* **Allons!** *Come (now)! Come on! Let's go!*
s'en aller: (vintr) (III) *to go out of, away*
  Allez vous-en! *Get out!*

allumer (vtr) (i) *to light*; *to set fire to*

allumette, une (n) *match* [for lighting]

alors (adv) *then*; *at that time*

alphabet, un (n) *alphabet*

amener (vtr) (I, OC, 1) *to lead, to bring*

ami, un, une amie *friend, boy/girl friend*

amour, un (*n*) *love*

amusant, -e (adj) *amusing, entertaining*

amuser (vtr) (I) *to amuse, to entertain*

s'amuser (vintr) (I) *to amuse, to enjoy oneself*

an, un (n) *year*
en l'an 1968 *in the year 1968*

année, une (n) *year* [period of time]
pendant deux années *for two years*

ancien, -ne (adj) *ancient, old; former*
un ancien combattant *an ex-serviceman*

âne, un; une ânesse (nm & f) *donkey, ass*

animal, un (pl) **animaux** n *animal*

appareil, un (n) *apparatus, device, appliance; machine*
un appareil photo *camera*
un appareil radio *radio set*

appartement, un (n) *flat, suite of rooms*

appeler (vtr) (I, OC, 3) *to call, call out*
s'appeler *to be called, named*

apporter (vtr) (I) *to bring (to)*

apprendre (vtr) (III) *to teach*
— (vintr) *to learn*

après (prep or adv) [place, time] *after; afterwards*
Il est parti après moi (prep)
Je suis parti après (adv)

après-midi, un (n) *afternoon*

arbre, un (n) *tree*

argent, l' (nm) *silver* [metal]; *money*

arme, une (n) *weapon*

armée, une (*n*) *army*

armoire, une (n) *wardrobe; cupboard*

arranger (vtr) (I, OC, 2) *to arrange; to tidy up*
s'arranger *to manage*

arrêt, un (n) *stop, halt*

arrêter (vtr) (I) *to stop; to arrest*
s'arrêter (vintr) *to stop*

arrière, l' (nm) *back, rear*
à l'arrière *at the back*

arrière (adj, prep & adv) *behind; backwards*
aller en arrière *to go backwards*
en arrière de (adv) [place] *behind*
faire marche arrière *to reverse* [a car]

arriver (vintr) (I) *to arrive (at à)* [with être]

art, un (n) *art*

artiste, un, une (nm & f) *artist; performer*

s'asseoir (III) *to be seated; to take a seat*

assis, -e (adj) *seated*

assez (adv) *enough (of* de)

assiette, une (n) *plate* [at table]

assuré, -e (adj) *firm, sure*

atelier, un (n) *workshop, workroom, artist's studio*

attacher (vtr) (I) *to attach, to tie, to fasten, to bind*

attendre (vtr) (III) *to wait (for), to expect*

attention, l' (nf) *attention*
faire attention *to pay attention, to be careful*
Attention! *Attention! Look out!*

au (art ms) *at the, to the*

aux (art m & f pl) See p. 15

aujourd'hui (adv) *today*

au revoir (adv) *good-bye*; *until we meet again*

aussi (adv) *also*; *as, so*
  aussi grand que *as big as*
  moi aussi *I also, I too*

aussitôt (adv) *immediately*

autant (adv) *as much, as many*
  — que *as much, many as*

auto, une (n = une **automobile**) *car, motor-car*

(auto)bus, un (n) *omnibus, bus*

(auto)car, un (n) *motor-coach*

auto-stop l' (nm) *hitch-hiking*
  faire de l'auto-stop *to hitch-hike*

automne, un or **une** (n) *autumn*

autour (adv) *round*

autour de (prep) *around* (something)

autre, -s (indef adj sing & pl) *other, others*

autre, un (indef pr) *another*
  d'autres (pl) *others*
  l'autre, les autres (pron) *the other, the others*
  autre chose *something else, another matter*

autrefois (adv) *formerly*

autrement (adv) *otherwise, differently*

autre part (adv) *somewhere else*

avancer (vtr) (I) *to move forward*
  s'avancer (vintr) (I) *to move forward to, towards*
  elle s'avance vers moi *she is moving towards me*

avant, un (n) *forepart, front part*

avant (prep or adv) *before* [time & space]
  avant midi *before noon*
  avant l'église *before (you to get to) the church*

en avant (prep & adv) *in front*
  En avant! *Forward!*

avant que (conj) *before*

avec (prep) *with*

avenue, une (n) *avenue*

aveugle (adj) *blind*

aveugle, un (n) *blind man.* **une aveugle** *blind woman*

avertir (vtr) (II, with **-ss-**) *to let know, to warn*

avenir l' (nm) *future*
  à l'avenir *in (the) future*

avion, un (n) *aeroplane*
  par avion *by plane*

avis, un (n) *opinion, advice, notice, news, warning*
  à mon avis *in my opinion*

avoir (vaux) *to have.* See p. 48
  avoir l'air *to look, to seem*
  avoir l'air malade *to look ill*
  avoir froid, chaud *to be cold, warm.* For other idioms in which **avoir** = English *to be*, see p. 54
  y avoir *there to be*
  il y a *there is.* See p. 54

avril (nm) *April*

B

bain, le (n) *bath*
  prendre un bain *to take a bath*

baiser, le (n) *kiss*

baisser (vtr) (I) *to lower*
  se baisser (vintr) *to bend, to stoop*

balai, le (n) *brush, broom*

balayer (vtr) (I, OC, 4) *to sweep, to brush*

balle, la (n) *ball, bullet*

banc, le (n) *bench*

banque, la (n) *bank* [for money, etc.]

barbe, la (n) *beard*

bas, le (n) *stocking; lower part (of de)*

bas, -se (adj) *low*

bas (adv) *low, down*

bateau, le pl **-x** (n) *boat, ship*
  un bateau à vapeur *steamship*
  —à voiles *sailing ship*
bâtiment, le (n) *building*
bâton, le (n) *stick, rod*
battre (vtr) (III) *to beat*
  se battre *to fight*
beau, bel, belle (adj) *beautiful*
  faire beau *to be fine* (weather)
  une belle *a beauty* (f)
beaucoup (adv) *much*
  il a beaucoup d'argent *he has a lot of money*
  beaucoup de gens *many people*
bébé, le (n) *baby*
bec, le (n) *beak, bill* [of bird]
bénéfice, le (n) *profit, earnings, benefit*
besoin, le (n) *need, want*
  avoir besoin (de) *to need*
bête, la (n) *beast, animal, creature*
  les petites bêtes *insects*
  bête noire *pet aversion*
bête (adj) *stupid, silly*
beurre, le (n) *butter*
  faire son beurre *to make one's pile*
bibliothèque, la (n) *library*
bicyclette, la (n) *bicycle*
  aller à bicyclette *to cycle*
bien (adv) *well*
  aller bien *to be well*
  ça va bien, je vais bien *I am well*
bientôt (adv) *soon*
  À bientôt *See you soon*
bijou, le pl **-x** (n) *jewel*
billet, le (n) 1. *note, short letter*
  un billet doux *love letter*
  2. *banknote, bill.* 3. *ticket*
  un billet de cinéma, théâtre *a ticket for the cinema, theatre*
  un billet simple *one-way ticket* [rail, bus, ship, air]. **un billet d'aller et retour** *return ticket, round-trip ticket*

bizarre (adj) *odd, strange, quaint*
blanc, blanche (adj) *white*
blé, le (n) *wheat*
blesser (vtr) (I) *to wound, to injure, to hurt*
  se blesser *to injure oneself, to hurt oneself*
blessure, la (n) *wound, injury*
bleu, -e (adj) *blue*
blouse, la (n) *smock, overall*
bœuf, le (n) *ox, beef* [pronounce the f] pl **les bœufs** [fs silent] *oxen*
boire (vtr) (III) *to drink*
bois, le (n) *wood* [timber]1. **du bois** *a piece of wood.* 2. **un bois** *a wood*
boisson, la (n) *drink*
boîte, la (n) *box*
  une boîte aux lettres *a letter-box*
boiteux, boiteuse (adj) *lame*
bon, bonne (adj) *good*
  une bonne *maid, servant*
  — d'enfant *nursemaid*
  une bonne femme *an old woman*
bonjour, le (n) *good morning, good day, good afternoon. Hello*
  dire bonjour à *to greet*
  donner le bonjour à *to give one's regards to*
bonsoir, le (n) *good evening*
bord, le (n) *side, brim, edge, brink*
  au bord de *beside, at the edge of*
bordeaux, le (n = vin de Bordeaux) *claret*
bouche, la (n) 1. *mouth* [pers] 2. *entrance*
  une bouche d'incendie *fire hydrant*
boucher (vtr) (I) *to block up, to plug*
boucher, le (n) *butcher*
  la bouchère *butcher's wife*
boucherie, la (n) 1. *butcher's shop* 2. *butchery, slaughter*

bouillir (vintr) (III, no -ss-) *to boil*

boue, la (n) *mud, filth*

bouger (vintr) (I) *to stir, to budge, to move, to fidget*

boulanger, le (n) *baker*
  la boulangère (n) *baker's wife*

boulangerie, la (n) *baker's shop*

bout, le (n) 1. *end, tip* 2. *bit, piece, chunk, butt* [of cigarette]
  au bout de la table *at the end of the table*

bouteille, la (n) 1. *bottle* 2. *cylinder*
  une bouteille d'oxygène *a cylinder of oxygen*

boutique, la (n) *(small) shop*

bouton, le (n) 1. *button* 2. *pimple*

branche, la (n) *branch* [of tree], *bough*

bras, le (n) *arm*

brave (adj) 1. *brave, bold* [after the noun] 2. *good* [before noun]

brique, la (n) *brick*

brosse, la (n) *brush*
  une brosse à habits *clothes-brush*
  — à cheveux *hairbrush*
  — à dents *toothbrush*

brouillard, le (n) *fog, mist*
  il y a du brouillard *it is foggy*

bruit, le (n) *noise*
  sans bruit *quietly*

brûler (vtr) (I) *to burn*
  se brûler *to burn oneself*

bureau, le (n) 1. *desk* 2. *office, bureau*
  le bureau de poste *post office*
  — de tabac *tobacconist's*
  — de renseignements *information office*

C

ça abbr **cela** (dem pron) *that*
  fam for *cela*. **je n'aime pas ça** *I don't like that, it*

Ça, par exemple! *Well, what do you know about that!*

Ça va? = **Comment allez-vous?**
  Ça va bien = **Je vais bien**
  C'est ça *That's it, agreed*
  ça et là *here and there*

cabinet, le (n) 1. *small room*; pl
  les cabinets *toilet, W.C.*
  2. **cabinet (de travail)** *study, lawyer's office (chambers), doctor's consulting room*

cacher (vtr) *to hide*
  se cacher *to hide oneself*

café, le (n) 1. *coffee* 2. *café, restaurant, public house*

calme (adj) *calm, still*

camarade, le, la (n) *comrade, pal*

camion, le (n) *lorry*

camionneur, le (n) *lorry driver*

campagne, la (n) *country, field*
  à la campagne *in the country*

camper (vintr) (I) *to camp, to set up camp*

camping, le (n) *camping*
  faire du camping *to go camping*

caoutchouc, le (n) *rubber (substance)*

car, 1. (conj) *for, because* 2. **le** (n) short for **autocar** = *coach*

carré, le (n) *square* [maths]

carré, -e (adj) *square, square-built*
  une table carrée *a square table*

carte, la (n) 1. *card* 2. **les cartes** *playing-cards* 3. *menu* 4. *map, chart*
  une carte postale *postcard*
  la carte d'identité *identity card*
  la carte des vins *wine list*

cas, le (n) *case, event, situation*

casser (vtr) (I) *to break, to smash*
  casser la croûte *to have a snack*
  casser la figure *to beat up*
  casser sa pipe (pop) *to die*

casserole, la (n) *saucepan*

cause, la (n) *cause, motive*
  à cause de *because of*

causer (vtr) (I) 1. *to cause* 2. *to chat*

causeur, -euse (adj) *talkative, chatty* (nm & f) *chatterbox*

cave, la (n) *cellar*

ce, cet (dem adj m sing) *this, that*

cette (f sing) *this, that*

ces (pl) *these, those.* See p. 25

ce, c', ceci, cela (dem pron) *this, that*

ceinture, la (n) *belt, sash, waist*

celui (dem pron m sing) *that*

celle (f sing) *that*

celles (f pl) *that*

ceux (m pl) *that of.* See p. 36

— -ci (adv) *here.* Joined to nouns preceded by **ce, cet, cettes, ces** and to dem pron **celui, celle, ceux, celles.** See **-là.** And p. 36

cent (num adj) *one hundred (100)*
Note: **deux cents francs** = *200 F.*
trois cent vingt francs = *320 F.*

centaine, une (n) *(about) a hundred*

centre, le (n) *centre, middle*

certain, -e (adj) 1. after noun *certain, positive, sure.* **un fait certain** *a positive fact* 2. before noun *some, certain.*
certaines choses *certain things, some things*

cesser (vtr) (I) *to stop, to cease*

chacun, chacune (indef pron) 1. *each* 2. *every one, everybody*

chaise, la (n) *chair*

chambre, la (n) *room.* Often used for **chambre à coucher** *bedroom*

champ, le (n) *field.* **les champs** *open country*

chance, la (n) *chance, luck*
avoir de la chance *to be lucky*
Quelle chance ! *What luck !*

changer (vtr) (I, OC, 2) *to change, to exchange*

changer de l'argent *to change money*

se changer *to change one's clothes*

chanson, la (n) *song*

chant, le (n) *singing, song*

chanter (vtr) *to sing*
le coq chante *the cock crows*

chapeau, le pl **-x** (n) *hat*

chaque (indef adj) *each*
chaque fois *each time*

charge, la (n) 1. *load, burden* 2. *dependent, charge, care*
Il est à ma charge *He is in my care* (= *he is a dependent*)

chargé, -e (adj) *full, loaded* [of camera, gun, etc.]

charger (vtr) (I) 1. *to load* 2. *to entrust with*
se charger (de) *to take on, to see to something*
je m'en charge *I'll see to it*

charmer (vtr) (I) *to charm*

charrue, la (n) *plough*

chasse, la (n) *chase, hunt, hunting*

chasser (vtr) (I) 1. *to hunt* 2. *to chase, to drive*

chasseur, le (n) *hunter, porter, page-boy* [hotel]

chat, le (n) *cat*
chatte, la (nf) *cat*

chaud, -e (adj) *warm, hot*
avoir chaud *to be hot* [pers]
faire chaud *to be hot* [weather]

chauffage, le (n) *heating*
le chauffage central *central heating*

chauffer (vtr) (I) *to heat, to warm*
chauffer le moteur *to warm up the engine*
se chauffer *to get warm, to warm oneself* (**au feu** *at the fire*)

chauffeur, le (n) *chauffeur, driver* [of car], *fireman, stoker* [of steam engine]

chaussée, la (n) *road, street* [as opposed to pavement]
chaussette, la (n) *sock*
chaussure, la (n) *shoe*
chef, le (n) *head, chief, leader*
— **de famille** *head of family*
— **de train** *guard* [on a train]
— **de cuisine** *chef* (*chief cook*)
— **d'équipe** *captain* [of a team], *team leader*
— **de gare** *stationmaster*
 l'ingénieur-en-chef *chief-engineer*
chemin, le (n) *way, route, road, path*
  ce chemin va à Paris *this road goes to Paris*
  chemin de fer *railway*
chemise, la (n) 1. *shirt* (men) 2. *folder, jacket* (*filing*)
  chemise de nuit *nightdress*
cher, chère (adj) 1. *dear, beloved* 2. *dear, costly, expensive*
chercher (vtr) (I) 1. *to look for, to seek* 2. **+à** *to try to*
  aller chercher *to go and get, to fetch*
cheval, le pl **les chevaux** (n) *horse*
  à cheval 1. *on horseback* 2. *astride*
  à cheval sur une branche *astride a branch*
cheveu, le (n) *single hair*
cheveux, les (n) *hair* [of the head]
chèvre, la (n) (*she-*) *goat*
chez (prep) 1. *at the home of, at someone's place.* **chez**+ disj pron. **chez moi** *at my place.* **chez soi** *at one's* (*own*) *place* 2. *with*: **il habite chez les Jones** *he lives with the Joneses* 3. *among*: **chez les Français** *among the French* (*people*)
  avoir un chez-soi *to have a home of one's own*
chic, le (n) *skill, knack, style*

 avoir du chic *to have style* (adj inv) *stylish*
 un chic type (fam) *a good bloke*
chien, le, la chienne (n) *dog, bitch*
chiffon, le (n) *rag, cleaning cloth, duster*
chiffre, le (n) *number, figure* [1, 2, 3]
chocolat, le (n) *chocolate*
  du c. au lait *milk chocolate*
choisir (vtr) (II) *to choose, to select*
choix, le (n) *choice*
chose, la (n) *thing, object, matter, affair*
  quelque chose (indef pron) *something*
chute, la (n) *fall*
  faire une chute *to fall*
ciel, le, pl **les cieux** *sky*
  les cieux [in paintings] *the heavens*
  le ciel [religion] *heaven*
cigare, le (n) *cigar*
cigarette, la (n) *cigarette*
cimetière, le (n) *cemetery*
cinéma, le (n) *cinema*
  aller au c. *to go to the cinema*
cinq (num adj) *five* (*5*)
cinquante (num adj) *fifty* (*50*)
circuler (vintr) (I) *to move about* (vtr) *to pass round something*
ciseaux, les (npl) *scissors*
clair, -e (adj) 1. *bright* [of light] 2. *light* [colour]
  au clair de lune *by moonlight*
classe, la (n) *class, classroom*
  en classe *in class* [at school]
client, le, la cliente (n) *client, customer*
clef, la (or **la clé**) (n) *key*
clou, le (n) *nail* [carpentry]
club, le (n) *club* [social]
cochon, le (n) *pig*
code, le (n) *code*
  code de la route *highway code*

cœur, le (n) 1. *heart* 2. *middle, core centre* [of something]
  avoir mal au cœur *to feel sick*
  avoir bon cœur *to be kind-hearted*
  par cœur *by heart*
coiffeur, -euse (nm & f) *hairdresser*
coiffure, la (n) *hair style*
coin, le (n) *corner*
  au coin de la rue *at the street corner*
colère, la (n) *anger*
  être en colère *to be angry*
collège, le (n) *secondary school*
combien (inter adv) *how much, many*
  combien font 2+3+4? *how many are 2 plus 3 plus 4?*
commande, la (n) 1. *order* [for sth] 2. *command* [of army]
commander (vtr) (I) *to command* [in army], *to order*
  commander un repas *to order a meal*
comme (conj or adv) 1. *like, as* 2. *because, as*
  (adv) **comme il fait beau!** *how fine it (the weather) is!*
commencement, le (n) *beginning*
commencer (vtr) (I, OC, 2) *to begin*
  il commence à pleuvoir *it is beginning to rain*
comment? (inter adv) *how?*
  comment allez-vous? *how are you?*
commerçant, le (n) *tradesman, merchant, shopkeeper*
commerce, le (n) *trade, commerce*
comprendre (vtr) (III, like **prendre**) 1. *to understand* 2. *to comprise*
compte, le (n) *count, reckoning, amount, account*
  comptes, les (npl) *accounts* [book-keeping]

compter (vtr) (I) *to count, to reckon, to number*
  compter sur *to count (rely) on*
concierge, le, la (n) *doorkeeper, caretaker*
conduire (vtr) (III) 1. *to drive* (car) 2. *to lead, to conduct, to guide*
congé, le (n) 1. *holiday, leave* 2. *dismissal*
connaître (vtr) (III) *to know, to be acquainted with* [a person]
connu, -e (adj) *known*
conseil, le (n) 1. *(piece of) advice* 2. *councillor, consultant*
  le conseil municipal *the municipal, local, council*
construction, la (n) *building, construction*
construire (vtr) (III, p. 61, like **conduire**) *to build, to construct*
construit, -e (adj) *built*
contenir (vtr) (III, like **tenir**) *to contain, to hold*
content, -e (adj) *glad, pleased*
continuer (vtr) (I) 1. *to continue* 2. *(vintr) to extend, to go on, to keep on*
contrat, le (n) *contract*
contraire (adj) *contrary, opposite*
contre (prep) *against* (adv) *near*
  contre le mur *near* (or *against*) *the wall*
contrôle, le (n) 1. *roll* 2. *inspection point* 3. *control*
contrôler (vtr) (I) *to control, inspect, check, supervise*
contrôleur, -euse (n) *inspector, supervisor*
coq, le (n) *cock*
corde, la (n) *cord, rope, line*
cordonnier, le (n) *shoemender, cobbler*
corps, le (n) 1. *body* 2. *main point*
corsage, le (n) *blouse*

côté, le (n) *side*
  à côté (de) (prep) *beside*
  à côté (adv) *beside, near*
côte, la (n) 1. *coast, shore* 2. *rib, side* 3. *slope, hill*
coton, le (n) *cotton*
cou, le (n) *neck*
coucher (vtr) (I) *to put to bed*
  se coucher *to go to bed, to lie down*
coudre (vtr) (III) *to sew*
couler (vintr) (I) 1. *to run, to flow, to slip by, to leak* 2. *to slide down, to sink*
couleur, la (n) *colour*
coup, le (n) *blow, knock, rap*
  coup de pied *kick*
  coup de vent *gust of wind*
couper (vtr) (I) *to cut*
cour, la (n) *court, courtyard*
courage, le (n) *courage, bravery*
courir (vintr) (III) *to run*
course, la (n) 1. *race* 2. *course*
  les courses *the races*
court, -e (adj) *short*
cousin, le, cousine, la (n) *cousin*
cousu, -e (adj) *sewn, sewed*
couteau, le pl -x (n) *knife*
coûter (vtr) (I) *to cost*
couvercle, le (n) *lid, cover*
couverture, la (n) *covering, cover*
  couverture de lit *bedspread*
couvrir (vtr) (III) *to cover*
cracher (vtr) (I) *to spit*
cravate, la (n) *tie*
crayon, le (n) *pencil*
creuser (vtr) (I) *to excavate, to scoop out, to dig*
creux, creuse (adj) *hollow*
crier (vintr) (I) *to shout, to cry out*
croire (vtr) (III) *to believe*
cru, -e (adj) *raw*
cueillir (vtr) (III) *to gather, to pluck*
cuiller, la (n) *spoon*

cuir, le (n) *skin* [of animals], *leather*
cuire (vtr) (III) *to cook*
cuisine, la (n) 1. *kitchen* 2. *cookery*
cuit, -e (adj) *cooked, baked* (fam) *very drunk*
culotte, la (n) *pants, shorts, knickers*
cultivateur, le (n) *farmer*
cultiver (vtr) (I) *to cultivate, to farm*
cultivé, -e (adj) *cultivated* [of the land] *cultivated* [of the mind], *educated*
culture, la (n) *culture, crop*
curé, le (n) *priest* [of village or parish]
curieux, -ieuse (adj) 1. *inquisitive* 2. *odd, curious*
cuvette, la (n) 1. *wash-basin, bowl* 2. *developing dish* [photography]

D

dame, la (n) *lady*
danger, le (n) *danger*
dangereux, -euse (adj) *dangerous*
dans (prep) *within.* See p. 66; *of time= at the end of*
  dans un mois *in a month*
danse, la (n) *dance, dancing*
danser (vintr) (I) *to dance*
danseur, le, danseuse, la (n) *dancer*
davantage (adv) *more, longer*
de (d') (prep) *of, from*
debout (adv) *upright, standing*
se débrouiller (vintr) (I) *to manage, to get along, to get out of* (*a difficulty*)
  il se débrouille mal *he is not managing very well*
début, le (n) *beginning*
  au début *at the beginning*
débuter (vintr) (I) *to start out, to begin*

décembre (nm) *December*

décharger (vtr) (I) *to unload*

déchirer (vtr) (I) *to tear, to tear up*

décider (vtr) (I) *to decide*

décorer (vtr) (I) *to decorate, to ornament*

déçu, -e (adj) *disappointed*

dedans (adv) *inside, within*

défendre (vtr) (III, like **descendre**) *to defend*

dehors (adv) *out, outside*
  en dehors de la maison *outside the house*
  le dehors *the outside*

déjà (adv) *already, previously*

déjeuner (vintr) (I) 1. *to breakfast* 2. *to lunch*

déjeuner, le (n) *lunch, midday meal*
  le petit déjeuner *breakfast*

demain (adv) *tomorrow*

demander (vtr) (I) *to ask, to request* [not to demand]
  se demander (vintr) *to wonder, to speculate about*

déménager (vintr) (I) *to move house*

demeurer (vintr) (I) 1. *to stop, to remain* 2. *to reside, to dwell*
  with { **être** *to stop, to remain* / **avoir** *to reside, to dwell*

demi, -e (adj) *half, semi-, half-*
inv + hyphen before the noun
  une demi-heure *half an hour*
  un demi-verre *half a glass*
  var. after noun
  une heure et demie *an hour and a half*

demoiselle, la (n) 1. *unmarried woman* 2. *young lady* 3. *assistant* (f)
  demoiselle de magasin *shop* [store] *girl, assistant*

démolir (vtr) (II, with **-ss-**) *to knock down, to demolish*

dent, la (n) *tooth*

7—B.E.F.

départ, le (n) *start, departure*

département, le (n) *one of the territorial counties of France*

dépenser (vtr) (I) *to spend*

dépêcher (vtr) (I) *to hurry, to expedite something*
  se dépêcher (vintr) *to make haste, to hurry*

déposer (vtr) (I) *to deposit, to put down*

depuis (prep) *since, for* [of time]
  depuis que + verb *since* + verb

déranger (vtr) (I) *to disturb, to trouble, to disarrange something*

dernier, -ère (adj) *last, latest*

derrière, le (n) *back, rear*

derrière (adv & prep) *behind, at the back of*

des (abbr for **de** + **les**) *of the*

descendre (vintr) (III, with **être**) *to go down* or *come down, to get out* [of a vehicle]

déshabiller (vtr) (I) *to undress*
  se déshabiller *to undress oneself*

désirer (vtr) (I) *to wish, to desire, to require*

dessin, le (n) *drawing, sketch(ing)*

dessiner (vtr) (I) *to draw, to sketch, to design, to lay out*

dessous (adv) *below, underneath*
  au-dessous de (prep) *below*

dessus (adv) *above, on, upon*

détester (vtr) (I) *to hate, to detest*

dette, la (n) *debt*

deux (num adj) *two* (2)

deuxième (adj) *second* (2nd)

devant (adv & prep) *before, in front of*
  le devant (n) *the front part*

développer (vtr) (I) *to develop*

devenir (vintr) (III like **venir**) *to become*

devoir, le (n) *duty, obligation, homework*

devoir (vtr) (III) 1. *to owe* 2(*a*) *to be supposed to* (*b*) *must*
+inf je dois partir *I must go*

diable, le (n) 1. *devil* 2. *scamp, rascal*

Dieu, le (n) *God*
  Dieu merci! *Thank heaven!*

différence, la (n) *difference*

différent, -e (adj) *different*

difficile (adj) *difficult*

difficulté, la (n) *difficulty, trouble*

dimanche, le (n) *Sunday*

dîner, le (n) *dinner*

dîner (vintr) (I) *to dine, to have dinner*

dire (vtr) (III) *to say* or *to tell*
  vouloir dire *to mean*

direct, -e (adj) *direct, through* [of a train]

directeur, le (n) *manager, director*
  directrice, la (n) *manageress*

direction, la (n) 1. *management* 2. *direction* 3. *driving* [of a car]
  un train en direction de Lyon *a train for Lyon*

discuter (vtr) (I) 1. *to discuss, to debate* 2. *to argue, to question, to dispute*

disque, le (n) *disc, record*

distingué, -e (adj) *distinguished, refined*

dix (adj) *ten* (*10*)

dixième (num adj) *tenth* (*10th*)

dizaine, la (n) (*about*) *ten*

docteur, le (n) *doctor*

doigt, le (n) *finger*

domestique (adj) *domestic* (n) *servant*

donc (conj) *therefore*

donner (vtr) (I) *to give*

dormir (vintr) (III) *to sleep*

dos, le (n) *back*

douche, la (n) *shower-bath*

double, le (n) *double*

double (adj) *double*

douleur, la (n) 1. *pain* 2. *grief*

doux, douce (adj) 1. *soft* 2. *sweet*

douze (num adj) *twelve* (*12*)

douzième (adj) *twelfth* (*12th*)

drap, le (n) *cloth, bed sheet*

drapeau, le (n) *flag, banner*

droit, le (n) *law, right*
  also: *tax, duty, royalty*

droite, la (n) *right* [hand, side]
  à droite *on the, to the right*

droit, -e (adj) *straight*

drôle (adj) *odd, funny*

du (abbr for **de + le**) *of the*

dû, due, dus, dues (adj) *owing*

dur, -e (adj) *hard, tough, harsh, difficult*

durée, la (n) *duration, period of*

durer (vintr) (I) *to last, to endure*

E

eau, une (n) *water*
  eau-de-vie *brandy*

échapper (vintr) (I) *to escape, to slip away, to elude*

échelle, une (n) *ladder, scale*

éclair, un (n) 1. *lightning, flash of light* 2. *small cream cake*

éclairer (vtr) (I) *to light up, to illuminate* sth

école, une (n) *school*

écouter (vtr) (I) 1. *to hear* 2. *to listen* (*to, in*)

écran, un (n) 1. *screen* 2. *filter* (photo.)

écraser (vtr) (I) *to crush, to bruise, to flatten*
  se faire écraser *to get run over*

écrire (vtr) (III) *to write*

écrit, -e (adj) *written*
  un écrit *a written document*

écriture, une (n) *handwriting*

écrivain, un (n) *writer, author*

édifice, un (n) *building*
effacer (vtr) (I, OC, 2) *to wipe, to rub out, to obliterate*
effort, un (n) *effort*
  sans effort *effortless(ly)*
égal, -e mpl **égaux** (adj) *equal*
électricité, l' (nf) *electricity*
électrophone, un (n) *record player*
élève, un, une (nm & f) *pupil, student*
élever (vtr) (I, OC, 1) *to raise, to elevate*
  s'élever (vintr) 1. *to rise up, to raise oneself* 2. *to work one's way up*
elle, elles (pers pron) *she, they* (f)
  à elle, à elles *hers, theirs* (f)
s'embarquer (vintr) (I) *to board* [ship, plane]
embrasser (vtr) (I) *to kiss, to embrace*
emmener (vtr) (I, OC, 1) *to lead, to conduct*
— avec *to take with*
empêcher (vtr) (I) *to prevent, to hinder*
employer (vtr) (I) *to employ*
employé, un, une employée (n) *employee, clerk, woman clerk*
emporter (vtr) (I) *to carry away, to take away*
  s'emporter *to lose one's temper*
en (prep) [time] *in, to, at, made of*
  en été *in summer*
  en or *made of gold*
  (adv) [place] **j'en viens** *I come from there*
  (pron) *of it, him, her,* etc. **j'en ai** *I have* (*some*) *of it.* See p. 66
encore (adv) *still, yet, more, again, furthermore*
  pas encore *not yet*
s'endormir (vintr) (III, like **dormir**) *to fall asleep*
endroit, un (n) *place, spot*

enfant, un, une (nm & f) *child*
enfin (adv) *finally, lastly, in short*
enlever (vtr) (I, OC, 1) *to remove, to take away*
ennemi, un, une ennemie (nm & f) *enemy*
ennui, un (n) 1. *worry, trouble* 2. *boredom*
ensemble (adv) *together, altogether* (nm) 1. *whole* 2. *cohesion*
ensuite (adv) *then, after that, afterwards*
entendre (III, like **vendre**) 1. *to hear* also *to listen* 2. *to understand*
enterrer (vtr) (I) *to bury*
entourer (vtr) (I) *to surround, to enclose*
entre (prep) *between, among(st)*
entrée, une (n) *entry, entrance, admission*
entrer (vintr) (I) *to go in, to enter* [with **être**]
enveloppe, une (n) *envelope, wrapper*
envie, une (n) *longing, desire*
  avoir envie de *to like to*
  j'ai envie de + v *I should like to, I fancy* (+inf)
envoyer (vtr) (III, takes **i** instead of **y** before e-mute) Fut
  j'enverrai *to send, to despatch*
épais, -se (adj) *thick*
épaule, une (n) *shoulder*
épicerie, une (n) *grocer's shop*
épicier, -ère (n) *grocer* m, f *grocer's wife, lady assistant in grocer's shop*
épingle (n) *pin*
épuisé, -e (adj) 1. *exhausted* 2. *sold out* 3. *out of print* [book]
escalier, un (n) *staircase*
équipe, une (n) *working-party, gang, team* [in sport]
espace, un (n) *space*
espérer (I, OC, 1) *to hope, to expect*

espoir, un (n) *hope*

esprit, un (n) *spirit, mind, wit*

essayer (vtr) (I, OC, 4) *to try, to try on, to test, to attempt*

essence, une (n) *petrol, gasoline*

essuyer (vtr) (I, OC, 4) *to wipe, to clean*

est, l' (nm) *east*

et (conj) [t always silent] *and*

   et ... et ... *both ... and ...*

étage, un (n) *storey, floor*

état, un (n) 1. *state, condition* 2. *statement, list, note*

été, un (n) *summer*

éteindre (vtr) (III, like **peindre**) *to extinguish, to put out* [light, fire]

étiquette, une (n) 1. *label, tag* 2. *etiquette, good manners*

étoile, une (n) *star*

étonner (vtr) *to astonish, to take by surprise, to amaze*

étranger, -ère (n & adj) *strange(r), foreign(er)*

être (vintr) (III) *to be* (See pp. 48–50)

   être à *to belong to*

   c'est à moi *it is mine*

   un être (n) *being, existence, living creature*

étroit, -e (adj) *narrow, tight*

étude, une (n) *study* [of sth]

   l'étude des langues *the study of languages*

étudiant, -e (n) *student*

eux (disj pron) *them*

   eux-mêmes *themselves*

événement, un (n) *event, happening*

éviter (vtr) (I) *to avoid, to dodge*

exact, -e (adj) *exact, correct*

excuser (vtr) (I) *to excuse* [sb, sth]

   s'excuser *to apologize*

examen, un (n) *examination, test*

exemple, un (n) *example, pattern*

   par exemple *for example*

Par exemple! *Upon my word!*

excellent, -e (adj) *excellent*

exister (vintr) (I) *to exist, to be*

expliquer (vtr) (I) *to explain*

extérieur, -eure (adj) *outer, exterior, external*

   à l'extérieur *outside* (**de** *of*)

extraordinaire (adj) *extraordinary, outstanding*

F

façade, la (n) *front, face* [of building]

face, la (n) *face, countenance*

   en face (adv) *opposite*

   en face de (prep) *opposite to*

   face à *facing*

fâché, -e (adj) *angry, cross*

facile (adj) *easy*

   facilement (adv) *easily*

facilité, la (n) *ease, facility*

façon, la (n) 1. *making, fashioning* 2. *way, manner*

   de toute façon *anyway, anyhow*

   de cette façon *this way*

   de façon que *so that*

facteur, le (n) *postman*

facture, la (n) *invoice, bill*

facultatif, -ve (adj) *optional, on request*

faible (adj) 1. *weak, feeble* 2. *faint, slight* [sound, light] 3. *small, inadequate*

faim, la (n) *hunger*

   avoir faim *to be hungry*

faire (vtr) (III) *to do, to make*

   faire froid, chaud *to be cold, warm* [of weather]

   faire + inf. *to cause sth to be done*: **faire bâtir une maison** *to have a house built*. **faire une promenade** *to take a walk*. See also p. 63

falloir (vimpers) (III, and p. 53) *to be necessary, to need, to lack* (obligation) *must*
  il me faut des francs *I need* (*lack*) *francs*
  il faut deux heures *it takes two hours*
  il nous faut partir *we must go*

famille, la (n) *family*

farine, la (n) *flour*

fatigue, la (n) *tiredness, fatigue*

fatigué, -e (adj) *tired*

fatiguer (vtr) (I) *to tire*

faute, la (n) *fault, mistake*

fauteuil, le (n) 1. *armchair* 2. *seat* [theatre, cinema]

faux, fausse (adj) 1. *false* (*erroneous*) 2. *false* (*deceitful*)

femme, la (n) 1. *woman* 2. *wife*

femelle, la (n) *female* [of animals only]

féminin, -e (adj) *feminine, female*

fenêtre, la (n) *window*

fer, le (n) *iron*
  le chemin de fer *railway*

ferme, la (n) *farm*

fermer (vtr) (I) *to shut, to close*

fête, la (n) *celebration, feast, fete, festival, saint's day*
  fête légale *legal holiday* (*Bank Holiday* in Britain)

feu, le (n) *fire*

feuille, la (n) *leaf* [of tree or book]

février (nm) *February*

fiancé, -e (adj or n) *betrothed, engaged*

ficelle, la (n) *string, twine*

fier, -ère (adj) *proud*

fièvre, la (n) *fever*

figure, la (n) *face, countenance*

fil, le (n) 1. *thread, yarn, fibre* 2. *wire* (= **fil de fer**)

filet, le (n) *net*
  filet à provisions *shopping bag*

fille, la (n) 1. *girl* 2. *daughter*

une jeune fille *girl, young woman* [a term to be preferred to **la fille**]

film, le (n) *film*
  un film muet *silent film*
  un film d'actualité *news-reel*

fils, le (pr fiss) (n) *son*

fin, la (n) *end*

finir (vtr) (II, with **-iss-**) *to finish*

fleur, la (n) *flower*

foin, le (n) *hay*

fois, la (n) *time, occasion*
  une fois *once.* **deux fois** *twice*
  trois fois, etc. *three times,* etc.
  à la fois *at the same time*
  la première fois, deuxième fois *first, second time*

foncé, -e (adj) *dark, deep* [colour]

fonctionnaire, le (n) *official, civil servant*

fond, le (n) 1. *bottom* 2. *back, far end* [of room, garden], *background* [of picture, landscape] 3. *subject-matter*

fondre (vtr) (III) *to melt, to smelt, to dissolve* [in cookery]
  (**je fonds, il fond, nous fondons, vous fondez, j'ai fondu, je fondrai**) **du beurre fondu** *melted butter*

force, la (n) *strength, force, vigour*

forcer (vtr) (I, OC, 2) *to force, to compel*

forcément (adv) *inevitably*

forêt, la (n) *forest*

forme, la (n) *form, shape*

former (vtr) (I) *to form, to shape, to create*

formidable (adj) 1. *formidable* 2. (pop) = *terrific, marvellous*

fort-e (adj) *strong, forceful*

fossé, le (n) *ditch, trench, drain*

fou, fol (m before a vowel or **h**-mute) **folle** (f) (adj) *crazy, mad, insane*

fou, le, la folle (n) *madman, mad woman, lunatic, crazy person*
foule, la (n) *crowd*
fourchette, la (n) *fork* [table]
fourneau pl. **-x** (n) *cooking stove*
  fourneau à gaz *gas-stove*
frais, fraîche (adj) *fresh, cool*
franc, franche (adj) *frank, sincere*
franc, le (n) *franc* [money]
France, la (n) *France*
français, -e (adj) *French*
  le Français *Frenchman*
  la Française *Frenchwoman*
frapper (vtr) *to strike, to hit, to knock* [at door]
frère, le (n) *brother*
froid, le (n) *cold*
  avoir froid *to feel cold*
  faire froid *to be cold* [weather]
fromage, le (n) *cheese*
front, le (n) 1. *forehead, brow* 2. *front* [of building] 3. *war front*
frontière, la (n) *frontier, boundary*
frotter (vtr) (I) *to rub, to polish, to strike* [a match]
fruit, le (n) *fruit*
fumée, la (n) *smoke*
fumer (vtr & intr) *to smoke*
furieux, -euse (adj) *furious, very angry or annoyed*
fusil, le (n) *gun, rifle*

G

gagner (vtr) (I) *to earn, to win, also to reach* [an objective]
gai, -e (adj) *gay, merry, bright, cheerful*
gant, le (n) *glove*
garçon, le (n) *boy, lad*
  garçon de café *waiter*
garage, le (n) *garage*
garagiste, le (n) *garage attendant*

garde, la (n) 1. *guard* 2. *custody* 3. *watch*
garde, le (n) *guard, keeper*
  garde- in compounds
garder (vtr) (I) *to keep, to protect, to retain, to guard*
gare, la (n) *railway station*
gâteau, le pl **-x** (n) *cake*
gauche (adj) 1. *left* 2. *awkward*
  à gauche *to the left, on the left*
gaz, le (pr z) (n) *gas*
gêner (vtr) (I, OC, 1) *to hinder, to cramp, to embarrass*
  se gêner 1. *to restrain onself* 2. *to inconvenience oneself*
genou, le pl **-x** (n) *knee*
genre, le (n) *kin, species, gender*
gens, les (nmpl) *people*
  de braves gens *good people*
gentil, -ille (adj) *pleasing, nice*
gilet, le (n) *waistcoat*
glace, la (n) 1. *ice* 2. *ice-cream* 3. *looking-glass*
goûter (vtr) (I) *to taste, to savour*
goutte, la (n) *drop, small quantity*
gouvernement, le (n) *government*
grade, le (n) 1. *rank* 2. *degree*
grain, le (n) *grain, corn*
graine, la (n) *seed of plants*
graisse, la (n) *fat, grease*
grand, -e (adj) 1. *big, tall* 2. *large* 3. *of note, importance*
  un homme grand *a big (tall) man*
  un grand homme *a great man*
  le grand-père *grandfather*
  la grand'mère *grandmother*
grandir (vintr) (II, with **-ss-**) *to grow, to get bigger, larger*
gras, -se (adj) 1. *fat, fatty* 2. *greasy, oily, thick*
grenier, le (n) 1. *attic* 2. *hay-loft, granary*
grève, la (*n*) *strike* [in industry]
gris, -e (adj) *grey*
  être gris, -e *to be tipsy*

gros, -se (adj) *big, bulky, stout*
grossir (vintr) (II, with -ss-) *to grow larger, bigger, to increase, to sell up*
groupe, le (n) *group*
gueule, la (n) 1. *mouth* [of animals] 2. (pop) = *mug* [of persons]
guérir (vtr) (II, with -ss-) *to cure* (vintr) *to become cured*
guéri, -e (adj) *cured*
guerre, la (n) *war*
guide, le, la (n) 1. *guide* [person] 2. *guidebook* [in m form]

H

habiller (vtr) (I) *to dress sb*
s'habiller *to dress oneself* [more common than se vêtir]
habit, un (n) *dress, costume*
les habits *clothes*
habitant, un (n) *inhabitant*
habiter (vtr) (I) *to inhabit, to live in*
habitude, une (n) *habit, custom, practice*
d'habitude (adv) *usually*
habituel, -le (adj) *usual, customary*
haut, le (n) *top, top part*
haut, -e (adj) *high, tall, lofty, upper, above*
(adv) *above.* **en haut** *at the top, upstairs*
hein? exclamation = n'est-ce pas? = *isn't it so?*
hein! *What!* [expresses incredulity]
herbe, une (n) 1. *grass* 2. *herb, plant*
mauvaises herbes *weeds*
heure, une (n) 1. *hour* 2. *o'clock* (See p. 31)
Quelle heure est-il? Il est une heure, deux heures
à l'heure *on time, per hour*

à tout à l'heure *see you soon, see you later*
heureux, -euse (adj) *happy, pleased*
heureusement (adv) *happily, luckily*
Heureusement! *A good thing too!*
hier (adv) *yesterday*
avant-hier *day before yesterday*
hier matin *yesterday morning*
hier soir *yesterday evening*
histoire, une (n) *history, story*
hiver, un (n) *winter*
homme, un (n) *man*
l'homme *mankind*
un jeune homme *young man, a youth*
*honte, la (n) *shame*
avoir honte *to be ashamed*
hôpital pl **-aux** (n) *hospital*
horloge, une (n) *clock*
hôtel, un (m) *hotel, mansion*
Hôtel de Ville *Town Hall*
hôtel meublé *residential hotel* [rooms, no board]
huile, une (n) *oil*
huit (num adj) *eight (8)*
huitième *eighth (8th)*
humide (adj) *damp, moist, humid*

I

ici (adv) *here*
idée, une (n) *idea, notion, whim*
Quelle idée! *The very idea!*
identité, une (n) *identity*
idiot, -e (adj) *idiotic, absurd*
un idiot (n) *a silly ass, fool*
il pl **ils** (pers pron) *he,* pl *they* (m)
île, une (n) *island*
image, une (n) 1. *picture* [in book, etc.] 2. *image, reflection, likeness*
important, -e (adj) *important*

impossible (adj) *impossible*
impôt, un (n) *tax, customs duty*
imprimé, -e (adj) *printed*
  un imprimé *printed matter, printed form*
incendie, un (m) *fire* [on a big scale]
inconnu, -e (adj) *unknown*
indiquer (vtr) (I) *to point out, to indicate*
industrie, une (n) 1. *industry*
  2. *activity*
industriel, -le (adj) *industrial*
  un industriel (n) *a manufacturer*
inférieur, -e (adj) *lower, inferior*
infirmier, un; une infirmière (n)
  male nurse; female nurse
ingénieur (n) *engineer*
information, une (n) *news (item)*
  les informations *the news*
insecte, un (n) *insect*
installer (vtr) (I) *to install, to set up*
  s'installer *to set up (shop), to install oneself, to settle in or down*
instrument, un (n) *instrument, tool*
intelligent, -e (adj) *intelligent*
intéressant, -e (adj) *interesting*
intéresser (vtr) (I) *to interest*
  s'intéresser à *to interest oneself in*
interdit, -e (adj) *forbidden, prohibited*
intérieur, -e *inside*
  à l'intérieur *on the inside*
inviter (vtr) (I) *to invite*
invité, -e un, une (n) *guest*

J

jamais (adv) 1. *never, not ever*
  2. *ever, for ever*
  Jamais! *Never!*
  ne + verb + jamais *never* (See p. 52)

jambe, la (n) *leg*
jambon, le (n) *ham*
janvier (nm) *January*
jardin, le (n) *garden*
jaune (adj) *yellow*
je, j' (pers pron) *I*
jeter (vtr) (I, OC, 3) *to throw* [takes tt before e-mute]
jeu, le (n) *game, play*
jeudi, le (n) *Thursday*
jeune (adj) *young*
  jeune homme pl **jeunes gens** *young man, young people*
  jeune fille *girl*
joie, la (n) *joy, mirth*
joli, -e (adj) *pretty, nice, attractive*
joue, la (n) *cheek*
jouer (vtr) (I) *to play*
jouet, le (n) *plaything, toy*
jour, le (n) *day, daylight*
journal pl **-aux** (n) 1. *newspaper*
  2. *diary* 3. *journal*
journée, la *day* [from morn till night], *daytime*
  une journée de travail *a day's work*
juif, juive (adj & n) *Jewish, Jew, Jewess*
juge, le (n) *judge, umpire*
juger (vtr) (I, OC, 2) *to judge, to be of opinion*
juillet (nm) *July*
juin (nm) *June*
jupe, la (n) *skirt*
jusque (prep) 1. [place] *up to, as far as*: **jusqu'ici** *up to here*
  2. [time] *till, until*:
  jusqu'aujourd'hui *until today*
  jusqu'en 1969 *until 1969*
juste (adj) 1. *just, fair, lawful*
  2. *correct, right*
  justement 1. *justly, properly*
  2. *precisely*
justice, la (n) 1. *justice* [legal]
  2. *fairness*

K

képi, le (n) *uniform cap* [military and police in France]

kilo (abbr for **kilogramme**) *(kg) kilogramme* (2·2 lb)

kilomètre (abbr km) = 1093 yards = 0·62 mile. 5 km = approx. 3 miles

L

l'
le ⎫ (def art sing) *the*
la ⎭

là (-**là**) (adv) *there* (See p. 36, dem pron)

là-bas (adv) *over there, yonder*

là-dedans (adv) *in that, in there*

là-dessous (adv) *under this, that, under there*

là-dessus (adv) *on this, on that*

là-haut (adv) *up there*

labourer (vtr) (I) *to till, to plough*

lac, le (n) *lake*

laid, -e (adj) *ugly*

laine, la (n) *wool*

laisser (vtr) (I) *to allow, to let, to permit*
  laisser + inf *to let sb do sth*
  laisser faire *to let do*
  laissez-le faire *let him do it, go ahead*
  laisser voir *to show*

lait, le (n) *milk*

lame, la (n) *blade* [of knife, razor]

lampe, la (n) 1. *lamp* 2. *radio valve*

lancer (vtr) (I, OC, 2) *to throw, to hurl, to launch*

langue, la (n) 1. *tongue* 2. *language*
  les langues vivantes *living (modern) languages*

large (adj) *broad, wide, ample*

lavabo, le (n) 1. *washbasin* 2. *washroom, toilet* (*W.C.*)

laver (vtr) (I) *to wash*
  se laver *to wash oneself, to have a wash*

le (art & pron) *the; him, it*

leçon, la (n) *lesson*

léger, -ère (adj) *light, slight*

légume, le (n) *vegetable*
  les légumes verts *green vegetables, greens*

lent, -e (adj) *slow*

lequel, laquelle, lesquels, lesquelles (1. adj & 2. rel pron) 1. *which* 2. *who, which*

les (art & pron pl) *the; them*

lettre, la (n) *letter*

leur, leurs (poss adj) *their*

leur (pers pron inv) *(to) them*

lever (vtr) (I, OC, 1) *to lift, to raise*
  se lever *to get up, to stand up, to get out of bed*

lèvre, la (n) *lip*

libraire, le (n) *bookseller*

librairie, la (n) *bookshop*

liberté, la (n) *freedom, liberty*

libre (adj) *free, vacant*

lieu, le pl -**x** (n) *place, spot, locality*

ligne, la (n) *line*
  écrire deux lignes à qn *to drop a line to sb*

limonade, la (n) *lemonade, soft drink*

lingerie, la (*n*) *underwear*

liquide, le (n) *liquid, fluid*

lire (vtr) (III) *to read*
  savoir lire *to know how to read*
  pouvoir lire *to see to read*

liste, la (n) *list, roll, register*

lit, le (n) *bed*

litre, le (n) *liquid measure* = 1*l* = 1·7 pints

livre, le (n) *book*

livre, la (n) *pound* (*lb*) *weight; pound* (£) *sterling*

logement, le (n) *lodging, billet, flat, apartment*

loi, la (n) *law*
  les lois du jeu *rules of the game*

loin (adv) *far*
  loin d'ici *far from here*
  aller trop loin *to go too far*

long, longue (adj) *long* [space and time]

longtemps (adv) *long, long time*
  il y a longtemps *long ago*

louer (vtr) (I) 1. *to hire out, to let a house* 2. *to praise*
  maison à louer *house to let*

lourd, -e (adj) 1. *heavy, ungainly, dull*

lui (pers pron) *he; him*
  lui-même *himself*

lumière, la (n) *light*

lundi, le (n) *Monday*

lune, la (n) *moon*

lunettes, les (nfpl) *spectacles, glasses*

M

ma (poss adj) *my*

machine, la (n) *machine, engine*
  la machine à écrire *typewriter*

maçon, le (n) *mason, bricklayer*

madame, mesdames (n) (Mme, Mmes) *Mrs*

mademoiselle, mesdemoiselles (n) (Mlle, Mlles) *Miss, Misses*

magasin, le (n) *(big) store, shop*
  grand magasin *big department store*
  en magasin *in stock*

magnétophone, le (n) *tape-recorder*

mai (nm) *May*

maigre (adj) *thin, lean*
  un maigre repas *a frugal meal*

main, la (n) *hand*

maintenant (adv) *now*

mairie, la (n) *Town Hall, mayor's office*

majeur, -e (adj) *major, important*

mais (conj) *but*

maison, la (n) *house, business firm, place, establishment*

maître, maîtresse (n) *master, mistress*
  maître d'école *schoolmaster*
  maître d'hôtel *head waiter*

mal, le, les maux (n) *hurt, harm, pain, evil*
  avoir mal à la tête *to have a headache*
  avoir le mal de mer *to be seasick*

mal = malade: il est très mal = il est très malade. faire mal (à) *to hurt, harm*

mal (adv) *badly*
  c'est mal écrit *it is badly written*

malade (adj) *ill, unwell, poorly*
  tomber malade *to fall ill*
  être malade *to be ill*

maladie, la (n) *illness, sickness, disease*

mâle (adj) *male*

malheur, le (n) *misfortune, unhappiness*

malheureux, -euse (adj) *unfortunate, unhappy, wretched*
  un malheureux (n) *an unfortunate man*

maman, la (n) *mama, mummy*
  grand'maman *grandma, granny*

manche, le (n) *handle* [of a tool, etc.]

manche, la (n) *sleeve*

Manche, la (n) *English Channel*

mandat, le (n) 1. *mandate* 2. *postal order, money order*
  le mandat-poste *postal money order*

manger (vtr) (I, OC, 2) *to eat*
  la salle à manger *dining-room*

manière, la (n) *manner, way of*
les manières *manners*
avoir de belles (mauvaises)
manières *to have good (bad)
manners*
de telle manière que + ind = *in
such a way that*
manquer (de) (vintr) (I) *to be short
of, to lack*
manquer de pain *to be short of
bread*
manteau, le pl -x (n) *overcoat,
cloak, mantle, wrap*
marchand, le, la marchande (n)
shopkeeper, storekeeper, dealer
marchandise, la (n) *goods, wares*
marché, le (n) *market*
le jour de marché *market day*
bon marché *cheap, good bargain*
marcher (vintr) (I) *to walk*
faire marcher qch *to make sth
work*
Ça marche? *How goes it? How
are things? Is it functioning?*
ma montre ne marche pas *my
watch has stopped*
mardi, le (n) *Tuesday*
mari, le (n) *husband*
marier (vtr) (I) *to marry, to marry
off*
se marier (vintr) *to get married*
marié, e (adj) *married.* (n) *married
person*
marmite, la (n) *saucepan, cooking-
pot*
marque, la (n) 1. *mark, sign*
2. *make, brand*
marquer (vtr) (I) 1. *to mark* 2. *to
brand*
mars (nm) *March*
marteau, le pl -x (n) *hammer*
masculin, -e (adj) *masculine, male*
matelas, le (n) *mattress*
matière, la (n) *matter, material*
matin, le (n) *morning*

un beau matin *a fine day*
de bon matin *early* [morning]
mauvais, -e (adj) *bad, wicked*
il fait mauvais temps *the weather
is bad*
la mer est mauvaise *the sea is
rough*
me (pers pron) *me*
mécanicien, le (n) *mechanic,
engine-driver, ship's engineer*
méchant, -e (adj) *bad, nasty,
vicious, naughty* [of a child]
médecin, le (n) *medical doctor*
médicament, le (n) *medicine*
meilleur, -eure (adj) *better*
le meilleur, la meilleure *the best*
membre, le (n) *limb, member* [of a
society]
mêler (vtr) (I) *to mix, to mingle, to
blend*
même (adj) 1. *same*: le même jour
the same day 2. *-self* (See p. 35)
moi-même *myself*
(adv) *even*: même lui *even he*
mémoire, la (n) *memory*
ménage, le (n) 1. *household*
2. *housekeeping, housework*
un jeune ménage *a young
married couple*
faire le ménage *to do the
housework*
une femme de ménage
charwoman
ménager, -ère (adj) *relating to the
house(hold).* article ménager
domestic appliance
la ménagère *the housewife*
mener (vtr) (I, OC, 1) *to lead, to
guide*
mensonge, le (n) *untruth, lie*
dire des mensonges *to tell lies*
mentir (vintr) (III, like sentir) *to
lie, to tell lies*
menu, le (n) *bill of fare, menu*
menuisier, le (n) *joiner*

mer, la (n) *sea*
  un homme à la mer! *Man overboard!*
merci, le (n) *thanks, thank you*
  Merci, oui *yes, please*
  Merci, non *no, thanks*
mercredi, le (n) *Wednesday*
mère, la (*n*) *mother*
mes (poss adj) *my*
mesure, la (n) *measure*
  fait sur mesure *made to measure*
mesurer (vtr) (I) *to measure*
métal, le pl **les métaux** *metal*
méthode, la (n) *method, system*
métier, le (n) *trade, occupation, craft, profession*
mètre, le (n) *metre* = 39·37 inches
  1m = 1 mètre = 100 centimètres
mettre (vtr) (III) *to put, to place*
  se mettre (vintr)
  se mettre en colère *to get angry*
  se mettre à table *to sit down at table*
  se mettre à + inf *to begin*
  il se met à travailler *he is starting to work*
meuble, le (n) *furniture, movables*
  les meubles *chattels, furniture*
meublé, -e (adj) *furnished*
  non meublé *unfurnished*
midi, le (n) *noon, south*
  le Midi *south of France*
mieux (adv) *better.* **le mieux** *the best*
mil (num adj) *1,000* [in dates only]
militaire (adj & n) *military, army* (n) *soldier*
mille (adj) *a thousand*
mille, le (n) *mile*
milieu, le pl **-x** (n) *middle* [time and space]
  au milieu de *in the middle of*
millier, un (n) *(about) 1,000*
milliard, un (n) *1,000,000,000*
million, un (n) *1,000,000*

mince (adj) *thin, slender*
minuit, le (n) *midnight*
minute, la (n) *minute*
mode, la (n) *fashion*
mode, le (n) *method, mode*
  le mode d'emploi *directions for use*
moderne (adj) *modern*
moi (pers pron) *I, me*
  à moi (poss): **c'est à moi** *it is mine*
moins (adv) *less, fewer, minus*
  moins d'argent *less money*
  moins d'hommes *fewer men*
  au moins *at least*
mois, le (n) *month*
moisson, la (n) *harvest*
  faire la moisson *to get the harvest in*
moitié, la (n) *half* (**de,** *of*)
moment, le (n) *moment*
  au moment où (*at*) **the moment when . . .**
  Un moment! *Just a moment!*
  à ce moment *at this moment*
mon (poss adj) *my*
monde, le (n) 1. *world* 2. *people*
  un homme du monde *a man of the world*
  beaucoup de monde *many people*
  tout le monde *everybody*
monnaie, la (n) 1. *change*
  2. *currency*
  la petite monnaie *small change*
  Avez-vous la monnaie de 1000 francs? *Have you the change of 1,000 francs?*
  la Monnaie *the mint*
monsieur, le, les messieurs (n) (abbr. **M., MM.**) *Mr, Messrs, sir*
  un monsieur *a gentleman*
  Used with 3rd pers sing verb:
  Monsieur a sonné? *Did you ring, sir?*

montagne, la (n) *mountain*

monter (vintr) (I) *to go up, to come up* [with être]

montre, la (n) *watch*

montrer (vtr) (I) *to show, to exhibit*

moquer (vtr) (I) *to mock sb, to ridicule*

se moquer (de) (vintr) *to mock, to make fun of*

vous vous moquez *you're joking*

morceau, le (n) *piece, slice*

mordre (vtr) (III) *to bite*

mordu, -e (adj) *bitten*

mort, la (n) *death*

mort, -e (adj) *dead*

mot, le (n) *word, saying*

un bon mot *joke, witticism*

mots croisés *crossword puzzle*

moteur, le (n) *engine*

moto, la (n) (abbr for motocyclette) *motor-bike*

mou, molle (adj) *soft, weak, flabby*

mol before vowel of mn

mouche, la (n) *fly*

un bateau mouche *small passenger boat* (on the River Seine)

mouchoir, le (n) *handkerchief*

mouiller (vtr) 1. *to wet* 2. *to drop anchor*

mouillé, -e (adj) 1. *wet* 2. *anchored*

mourir (vintr) (III) *to die* [with être]

moustique, le (n) *mosquito*

mouton, le (n) *sheep, mutton*

mouvement, le (n) *movement*

moyen, le (n) *means, medium*

les moyens *resources*

moyen, -ne (adj) *average, ordinary*

muet, -te (adj) *dumb, silent*

municipalité, la (n) *municipality, town council, local authority*

mur, le (n) *wall*

mûr, -e (adj) *ripe, mellow, mature*

musée, le (n) *museum*

musique, la (n) *music*

N

nager (vintr) (I, OC, 2) *to swim*

naïf, naïve (adj) *naïve, ingenuous, simple-minded*

naître (vintr) (III, with être) *to be born*

national, -e m pl -aux (adj) *national*

nationalité, la (n) *nationality*

nature, la (n) *nature, kind, character*

des pommes de terre nature *(plain) boiled potatoes*

du café nature *black coffee*

naturel, -le (adj) *natural*

naturellement (adv) *naturally, of course*

ne, n' (adv) *not*

ne ... negative particle:

ne ... pas *not*

ne ... que *only* (See p. 52)

ne ... jamais *never*

né, -e (pa part) *born* (of naître *to be born*) [with être]

il est né à *he was born at, in*

elle est née à *she was born at, in*

nécessaire (adj) *necessary*

nègre, le, la négresse (n) *Negro, Negress*

neige, la (n) *snow*

il tombe de la neige *it is snowing*

neiger (vimper) (I) *to snow*

il neige *it is snowing*

il a neigé *it (has) snowed*

il neigera *it will snow*

n'est-ce pas? *is it not so? isn't that so? true?*

net, -te (adj) 1. *clean, neat, distinct* 2. *nett*

nettoyer (vtr) (I, OC, 4) *to clean,*
to dust
   nettoyer à sec *to dry clean*
neuf (adj) *nine* (9)
neuf, neuve (adj) *new*
   Qu'y a-t-il de neuf? *What's new?*
neveu, le, la nièce (n) *nephew, niece*
nez, le (n) *nose*
ni ... ni ... (conj) *neither ...*
nor ...
   ni l'un ni l'autre *neither (of*
them)
Noël, le (n) *Christmas*
noir, -e (adj) *black*
noir, le (n) *(the) black, (the) dark*
nom, le (n) *name, noun*
   nom de famille *surname*
   nom de baptême *Christian name*
nombre, le (n) *number*
nombreux, -euse (adj) *numerous*
nommer (vtr) (I) *to name, to*
appoint
non (adv) *no*
   ni moi non plus *nor I either*
   non plus (adv) *neither*
nord, le (n) *north*
nos (poss adj) *our*
note, la (n) 1. *note* 2. *account, bill*
3. *school mark*
notre pl **nos** (poss adj) *our*
nôtre, -s with **le, la, les** (pron) *ours*
nous (pers pron) *we*
   nous-mêmes *ourselves*
   à nous: c'est à nous *it is ours*
nourriture, la (n) *food*
nouveau, nouvel (m before mn
vowel), **nouvelle** (adj) *new*
   la nouvelle *item of news*
   les (dernières) nouvelles *the*
(latest) news
novembre (nm) *November*
nu, -e (adj) *naked*
nuage, le (n) *cloud*
nuée, la, les nuées (n) 1. *cloud(s)*
2. *swarm, host*

nuit, la (n) *night*
nul, -le (adj) *nil, not any*
   nulle part (adv) *nowhere*
numéro, le (n) *number* [of house,
ticket, room, etc.], *issue* [of
periodical], *item* [on
programme, etc.]
nylon, le (n) *nylon*

O

objet, un (n) *object, thing*
obligatoire (adj) *obligatory,*
compulsory
obliger (vtr) (I, OC, 2) *to oblige, to*
compel
   obligé, -e *compelled, obliged,*
bound to [with **être**]
occasion, une (n) *occasion,*
opportunity
   d'occasion *second-hand*
occuper (vtr) (I) *to occupy, inhabit*
   occuper un appartement *to live*
in a flat
   s'occuper (de) *to go in for, to be*
interested in, to deal in
   occupé, -e (adj) *occupied, busy,*
employed, engaged
octobre (nm) *October*
œil, un, pl **les yeux** (n) *eye(s)*
œuf, un, pl **œufs** *egg*
[pr **f** in **œuf.** pr **les œufs** as **lez_œu**
f silent]
officiel, -le (adj) *official*
offrir (vtr) (III, like **ouvrir**) *to*
offer, to give
oiseau, un pl **-x** (n) *bird*
ombre, une (n) *shadow, shade*
   à l'ombre (de) *in the shade,*
shadow of
on (l'on) (indef pron) *one, they*
[+ verb in third pers s.
See p. 43]
oncle, un (n) *uncle*

ongle, un (n) *nail* [finger, toe]
onze (adj) *eleven* (*11*)
opération, une (*n*) *operation*
opinion, une (n) *opinion*
or, l' (nm) *gold*
orage, un (n) *thunderstorm*
ordre, un (n) *order, command, discipline*
  en ordre *in order*
  donner un ordre *to give an order, a command*
ordinaire (adj) *ordinary, common, usual*
oreille, une (n) *ear*
organe, un (n) 1. *organ* [of the body] 2. *medium, voice*
os, un (n) *bone* [pr s in sing, silent in pl: lez_o]
oser (vtr) (I) *to dare*
ôter (vtr) (I) 1. *to take away* 2. *to take off* [a garment]
ou (conj) *or*
  ou ... ou ... *either ... or ...*
où (rel pron & inter adv) *where, where?*
  d'où? *where from?* **par où? which way?**
  le jour où *the day on which*
oublier (vtr) (I) *to forget*
ouest, l' (nm) *west*
  à l'ouest *to, in the west*
oui (adv) *yes*
outil, un (n) *tool, implement*
ouvrage, un (n) *work, handicraft*
ouvrier, un, une ouvrière (n) *workman, workwoman.* **les ouvriers** *the workers*
ouvrir (vtr) (III) *to open*
ouvert, -e (pa part & adj) *open*
  ouvert la nuit *open all night*

P

page, la (n) *page*
paille, la (n) *straw*

pain, le (n) *bread, loaf*
  pain grillé *toast*
  petit pain (*French*) *roll*
  pain de savon *cake of soap*
  pain de sucre *loaf of sugar*
pair, -e (adj) *equal, even*
  au pair *with board and lodging but no pay*
  paire, la (n) *pair, couple*
paix, la (n) *peace*
  Paix! *Hush!*
  Laissez-moi en paix *Leave me alone*
panier, le (n) *basket*
pansement, le (n) (*medical*) *dressing*
pantalon, le (n) *pair of trousers, slacks*
papa, le (n) *daddy*
papier, le (n) *paper*
  papier à lettres *writing paper, notepaper*
  les papiers *personal documents* [passport, driving licence, identity card, etc.]
paquet, le (n) *packet, parcel, bundle*
par (prep) 1. *by:* **par erreur** *by mistake* 2. *through:* **par la porte, fenêtre** *through the door, window* 3. *on, in:* **par une belle journée** *on a fine day* (adv) **par avion** *by air, air mail*
  par ici, par là *this way, that way*
paraître (vintr) (III) *to appear*
  as impers: v: **il paraît** *it seems*
  il a paru *it seemed*
  il paraîtra *it will seem, appear*
parce que, qu' (conj) *because*
pardessus, le (n) *overcoat*
pardon, le (n) *pardon, forgiveness*
  Pardon! *I beg your pardon, sorry*
pardonner (vtr) (I) *to pardon, to forgive, to excuse*
  Pardonnez-moi! *Excuse me*

pareil, -le (adj) *like, alike, similar*
(nm) **le pareil, la pareille** *the
like, equal*

parent, le, la parente (n) 1. *parent*
2. *relation, relative*
les parents *parents, kinsmen*

parfait, -e (adj) *perfect*
Parfait! *All right!*

parfaitement (adv) *perfectly*
also *quite so, certainly, exactly*

parfois (adv) *at times, sometimes*

parler (vtr) (I) *to speak*

parole, la (n) *word, saying.* See **mot**
donner sa parole (d'honneur) *to
promise, to give one's word (of
honour)*

part, la (n) *part, share, portion*
pour ma part *as for me*

partager (vtr) (I) *to divide, to share
(out)*

particulier, -ère (adj) 1. *particular*
2. *peculiar*

partie, la (n) 1. *part* (of a whole):
la plus grande partie du chemin
the greater part of the way
2. *party;* as in **une partie de
plaisir** *party, outing* 3. *game,
match*: **une partie de football**
football match; **une partie de
tennis** *game of tennis*

partir (vintr) (III) *to go out, to set
out, to leave* [with **être**]
je suis parti *I left*

partout (adv) *everywhere*

pas, le (n) *step, stride, pace*
au pas *at walking pace, in step*
à chaque pas *at every step*
un faux pas *false step* [in
walking], *a social blunder*

pas (adv) **ne** + verb + **pas** *not*
pas un, une *not one*
pas moi *not I*
pas vrai? (pop) = **n'est-ce pas?** *is
it not so?*
pas du tout *not at all*

passage, le (n) *passage, journey,
thoroughfare*
Passage interdit *No
thoroughfare* [notice]

passager, -ère (n & adj) *passenger*
(m & f) (adj) *momentary,
fleeting*

passeport, le (n) *passport*

passé, -e (adj) *past, faded*
passé, le (n) *the past*

passer (vintr) (I) [with **avoir**
(action) and **être** (state)] 1. *to
go by, to pass by* 2. *to go by,
to come by* (**par**) 3. *to drop in
on sb*: **passer chez qn** 4. *of
time*: **le temps passe** *time
passes* (vtr) *to pass*: **passez-moi
le sel** *pass me the salt*
passer un examen *to take an
exam*
passer la journée *to spend the day*
se passer *to happen*

pâte, la (n) *paste, dough, batter*

pâté le (n) *pie, patty, meat paste*
pâté de foie *liver pâté*

patron, le, la patronne (n) *owner,
employer, boss, master,
mistress*

patte, la (n) *paw* [animals], *foot*
[of birds], *leg* [of insects]

pauvre (adj) *poor, needy, wretched*

paye, la (n) *wages* [workers], *pay*
[soldiers]

payer (vtr) (I, OC, 4) *to pay* (**je
paye** or **je paie**)

pays, le (n) *country, locality*
vin du pays *local wine*

paysan, le, la paysanne (n) *peasant*
(m & f) *small farmer, rustic*

peau, la (n) *skin, leather*

pêche, la (n) *fishing*
aller à la pêche *to go fishing*

pêcher (vtr) *to fish, to catch fish*

pêcheur, le (n) *fisherman*

peigne, le (n) *comb*

peigner (vtr) *to comb* (*out*)
  se peigner *to comb one's hair*
peindre (vtr) (III) *to paint*
peinture, la (n) 1. *painting* [art or action] 2. *paint* [material for painting]
  faire de la peinture *to go in for painting, to paint*
pelle, la (n) *shovel, spade*
pellicule, la (n) *roll of film*
pencher (vtr) (I) *to tilt*
  (vintr) *to lean, to incline*
  se pencher *to lean, to bend over*
  Ne pas se pencher au dehors *Do not lean out* [notice]
pendant (prep) *during*
  pendant que (conj) *while*
pendre (vtr & vintr) (III, like **vendre**) *to hang, to hang up, to be hanging*
pendu, -e (adj) *hanging (from* à*), hung, hanged*
penser (vtr & vintr) (I) *to think*
  penser à *to thing of* (tr) *sth*
  je pense que oui *I think so*
  je pense que non *I don't think so*
  Pensez donc! *Just think!*
pension, la (n) 1. *pension, allowance* 2. *payment for board and lodging* 3. **pension de famille** *boarding-house*
  être en pension chez *to be a boarder at*
perdre (vtr) (III) *to lose*
  perdre une partie (de) *to lose a game (of)*
  perdre son temps *to waste one's time*
  se perdre *to lose one's way*
perdu, -e (adj) *lost*
père, le (n) *father*
  (M.) Borderon père (*Mr*) *Borderon senior*
  le père Borderon *old man Borderon*

permettre (vtr) (III, like **mettre**) *to permit, to allow*
  Vous permettez? *May I?*
  Permettez! *Allow me!*
permis, -e (adj) *permitted*
  (n) **le permis** *permit*
personne, la (n) *person, individual*
  en personne *in person*
  être bonne personne *to be a good sort*
  personne (indef pron) *anyone, anybody, no one, nobody*
  Qui sonne? *Who is ringing?*
  Personne *Nobody*
peser (vtr & vintr) (I, OC, 1) *to weigh*
  (tr) **je pèse le paquet** *I weigh the parcel*
  (intr) **Le paquet pèse lourd** *the parcel weighs heavy*
petit, -e (adj) *small, little*
  un petit *a little boy*
  une petite *a little girl*
  les petits *the children, little ones*
  le petit-fils *grandson*
  la petite-fille *granddaughter*
  les petits-enfants *grandchildren*
pétrole, le (n) *petroleum*
  pétrole (lampant) *paraffin*
peu (adv) *little*
  (n) **un peu (de)** *a little (of)*
  à peu près (adv) *nearly, almost*
peuple, le (n) *people, nation*
peur, la (n) *fear*
  avoir peur *to be afraid*
  faire peur (à) *to make afraid, frighten*
  de peur de *for fear of*
  de peur que *for fear that*
peut-être (adv) *perhaps*
pharmacie, la (n) *pharmacy, chemist's shop*
pharmacien, le, la pharmacienne (n) *pharmacist chemist*

photo, la (= **la photographie**) (n)
  photo

photographie, la (n) *photography*
  faire de la photographie *to go in
    for photography, to take
    photos*
  photographier (vtr) (I) *to
    photograph*

pièce, la (n) *piece, part, patch*
  une pièce de monnaie *coin*
  une pièce de théâtre *play* [at
    theatre]
  une pièce de rechange *spare part*
  mettre une pièce *to put on a patch*
  une pièce *room* [in a house]

pied, le (n) *foot*

pierre, la (n) *stone*

pile, la (n) 1. *battery* 2. *pile, heap*
  pile sèche *dry cell*
  pile de rechange *refill* [battery]

pioche, la (n) *pick, pickaxe*

piocher (vtr) (I) *to dig with a pick*

pipe, la (n) *pipe, tube*
  il fume la pipe *he is a
    pipe-smoker*

piquer (vtr) (I) *to prick, to
    puncture, to sting, bite* [of
    insects]

piqûre, la (n) 1. *prick, sting, bite*
    2. *injection* [medical]
    3. *stitching*

pire (adj) = **plus mauvais** *worse*

pis (adv) = **plus mal** *worse*

pitié, la (n) *pity, compassion*
  avoir pitié de *to take pity on, to
    be sorry for*

place, la (n) 1. *place, position, seat*
    2. *circus* or *square* [street]
  Faites place! *Make way!*
  Place de la Concorde (*Square*)

plafond, le (n) *ceiling*

plaine, la (n) *plain, flat country*

plainte, la (n) *complaint*
  déposer une plainte contre *to
    lodge a complaint against sb*

plaire (à) (vtr) (III) *to please*
  s'il vous plaît *if you please, please*

plaisir, le (n) *pleasure*
  faire plaisir à *to please*
  cela me fait plaisir *that pleases me*
  avec plaisir *with pleasure*

planche, la (n) *plank*

plancher, le (n) *floor*

plante, la (n) *plant, shrub*

planter (vtr) (I) *to plant*

plat, -e (adj) *flat, level, even*
  tomber à plat *to fall flat*
  être à plat *to be 'flat out',
    exhausted*

plat, le (n) 1. *dish, course* [of a
    meal] 2. *flat* (*part of sth*)
  des œufs sur le plat *fried eggs*

plein, -e (adj) *full, filled, replete*

plein, le (n) *full, repletion*
  faire le plein *to fill up* [a tank
    with petrol]

pleurer (vintr) (I) *to weep, to shed
    tears, to cry*

pleuvoir (impers) *to rain*
  il pleut; il a plu; il pleuvra

plier (vtr) *to fold, to fold up, to
    bend*

pluie, la (n) *rain*

plume, la (n) 1. *feather* 2. *pen*
  le porte-plume *pen with nib* (See
    le stylo *fountain pen*)

plus (adv) *more (than* **que . . .**)
  plus grand que *greater, bigger
    than*
  plus de *more than* [before
    numerals]
  ne + verb + plus *no more, no
    longer*
  ni moi non plus *nor I either*
  plus tôt *sooner, earlier*

plusieurs (indef pron pl & adj)
    several, some

plutôt (adv) *rather*

pneu, le (n) *tyre*

poche, la (n) *pocket*

poêle, le (n) *stove*

poêle, la (n) *frying-pan*

poésie, la (n) *poetry*

poids, le (n) *weight*

  vendre au poids *to sell by weight*

poil, le (n) *hair of animals, hair of humans other than of head*

poing, le (n) *fist*

  un coup de poing *a blow with the fist*

point, le (n) 1. *spot, dot, mark, full stop* 2. *stitch*

pointe, la (n) 1. *point* [of a knife, etc.] 2. *tiptoe* **sur la pointe des pieds**

pointu, -e *sharp-pointed*

poisson, le (n) *fish*

poitrine, la (n) *chest, breast, bosom*

poli, -e (adj) 1. *polished, glossy* 2. *civil, courteous*

police, la (n) *police, constabulary* **un agent de police** *policeman*

politique (adj) *political* (n) **la politique** *politics, policy*

pomme, la (n) *apple*

pomme de terre, la (n) *potato*

pont, le (n) 1. *bridge* [on land] 2. *deck of ship*

port, le (n) 1. *port, seaport, harbour* 2. *postage, charges* 3. *carriage, carrying*

porte, la (n) *door, doorway, gate, entrance*

porte-cigarette, le (n) *cigarette-holder* pl **les porte-cigarettes**

porte-cigarettes, le (n inv) *cigarette case*

portefeuille, le (n) *wallet, portfolio*

porte-monnaie, le (ninv) *purse* pl **les porte monnaie**

porter (vtr) (I) *to carry, to bear, to wear* [clothes]

  se porter *to be in a state of health*: **je me porte bien** *I am well*

  je me porte mal *I am ill*

poser (vtr) (I) *to place, to pose, to put*

  poser une question *to ask a question*

posséder (vtr) (I, OC, 1) *to possess, to own*

possible (adj) *possible*

poste, le (n) *post, station*

  le poste de radio 1. *radio set* 2. *transmitting station*

poste, la (n) *postal service*

  le timbre-poste *postage stamp* pl **des timbres-poste**

pot, le (n) *pot, jug, jar, can*

  le pot-au-feu *boiled beef with vegetables*

  un pot de bière *mug of beer*

poule, la (n) *hen*

poulet, le (n) *chicken, young cock*

  la poulette *pullet*

pour (prep) *for*

  c'est pour moi *that's for me*

  partir pour Paris *to leave for Paris*

pourboire, le (n) *tip, gratuity*

pourquoi (inter adv) *why*

pousser (vtr) (I) *to push, to shove, to grow*

  pousser un cri *to utter a cry*

  (vintr) **l'herbe pousse** *the grass grows*

poussière, la (n) *dust*

pouvoir (vtr) (III) *to be able* [physically]

  il se peut *it can be, it may be, it's possible*

prairie, la (n) *meadow, prairie*

préférer (vtr) (I, OC, 1) *to prefer*

  je préfère le thé *I prefer tea*

préfet, le (n) *prefect* (*administrative head of a* **département**)

premier, -ère (adj) *first*

  la première fois *the first time*

  le premier ministre *prime minister*

prendre (vtr) (III) 1. *to take, to seize, to capture*
Common uses:
cela prend du temps *it takes time*
Prenez ce livre *Take this book*
je vais prendre un bain *I am going to have a bath*
je vais prendre le train pour . . . *I am going to take (catch) the train for . . .*
nous allons prendre froid *we are going to catch cold*
prendre l'air *to take the air, go for a stroll*

prénom, le (n) *first name, Christian name*

préparer (vtr) (I) *to prepare, to prepare for*
préparer un repas *to prepare a meal*

près (de) (adv & prep) *near*
c'est près *it is near*
prep: **c'est près de la poste** *It is near the post office*

présent, le (n) *present*

présent, -e (adj) *present*
être présent à *to be present at*
à présent *at present*
les présents *those present*

présenter (vtr) (I) *to introduce, to present* [a prize, etc.]
présenter son passeport *to show one's passport*
présenter qn à qn *to introduce sb to sb*: **je vous présente M. Dupont** *This is Mr Dupont*

presque (adv) *almost*

président, le (n) *president, chairman*

presse, la (n) *press, newspapers*

presser (vtr) (I) *to press, to squeeze*
se presser *to hurry, to hasten*

prêt, -e (adj) *ready, prepared*

prêter (vtr) (I) *to lend*

prêtre, le (n) *priest* [of any religion]

prévenir (vtr) (III, like **venir**) *to forewarn, to forestall*

prier (vtr) (I) *to request, to beseech*
je vous prie (de)+inf *I beg you to . . .*

printemps, le (n) *spring*
au printemps *in spring*

privé, -e (adj) 1. *private* 2. *deprived*

prix, le (n) 1. *price, cost, rate, worth, value* 2. *prize*

probable (adj) *probable*
probablement (adv) *probably*

prochain, -e (adj) *next, nearest*
lundi prochain *next Monday*
la prochaine ville *the next (nearest) town*

proche (adj) *near*

produire (vtr) (III, like **conduire**) *to produce, yield*

professeur, le, la (n) *teacher* [in secondary schools], *professor* [in a university]

profession, la (n) *profession, trade, calling*

profond, -e (adj) *deep, profound*

progrès, le (n) *progress*
faire du progrès *to make progress*

projectile, le (n) *projectile, missile*

promener (vtr) (I, OC, 1) *to take for a walk*
se promener *to go for a walk*

promenade, la (n) *walking, walk, outing*
faire une promenade à pied *to go for a walk*
faire une promenade en voiture *to go for a drive*

promettre (vtr) (III, like **mettre**) *to promise*

prononcer (vtr) (I) *to pronounce*

prononciation, la (n) *pronunciation*

propre (adj) 1. *own* 2. *clean, tidy, neat*
1 before n, 2 after: **mon propre mouchoir** *my own handk-*

erchief; **mon mouchoir**
   propre *my clean handkerchief*
propriétaire, le, la (n) *owner*
provision, la (n) *stock, stock in*
   hand
  les provisions *supplies, shopping*
  faire des provisions *to lay in a*
   store (supply) of
province, la (n) *province*
public, le (n) *the public*
public, publique (adj) *public*
puis (adv) *then, next, afterwards*
puits, le (n) *well, hole*
  l'eau de puits *well water*
punir (vtr) (II, with **-ss-**) *to punish*
puni, -e (adj) *punished*
pur, -e (adj) 1. *clear, pure* 2. *pure,*
  innocent

Q

quai, le (n) 1. *station platform*
  2. *quay, wharf*
qualité, la (n) *quality*
quand (conj) *when*
  (inter adv) **quand?** *when?*
quand même (adv) *even though,*
  even if, just the same
  je le ferai quand même *I will do*
   it just the same
quant à (prep) *as for, in regard to*
quarante (num adj) *forty (40)*
quart, le (n) *quarter, fourth part*
  un quart d'heure *a quarter of an*
   hour
  il est trois heures et quart *it is*
   3.15 (a quarter past three)
quartier, le (n) *district,*
  neighbourhood [town, city]
quatorze (num adj) *fourteen (14)*
quatre (num adj) *four (4)*
quatre-vingts (num adj) *eighty (80)*
quatre-vingt-dix (num adj) *ninety*
  (90)

que (adv) *only*
  je n'en ai que deux *I have only*
   two (of them)
que (conj) *that*
  il dit que vous partez *he says*
   that you are going
  il dit que oui *he says yes*
  Qu'il fait beau! *How fine it is!*
   [of weather]
que (rel pron) *whom, that, which*
  (often omitted in English,
  never in French): **l'homme**
  que j'ai vu *the man (whom) I*
  saw
  la lettre que j'ai écrite *the letter*
   (that, which) I wrote (See p. 41)
que? (inter pron) *what?*
qu'est-ce que c'est? *what is it?*
quel, quels, quelle, quelles (inter
  adj) *what? what sort of?*
quelque pl **quelques** (adj) *some, few*
  il y a quelque temps *some time*
   ago
  quelques jours *some, a few days*
quelqu'un, une ⎫
quelques-uns, -unes ⎬ (indef pron)
  (s) *someone, somebody, anyone,*
   anybody
  (pl) *some, any, a few*
quelque chose (indef pron)
  something
quelquefois (adv) *sometimes*
qu'est-ce qui? *what?* (**qui** =
  subject)
qu'est-ce que? *what?* (**que** =
  object)
question, la (n) *question*
  poser une question *to put, ask, a*
   question
queue, la (n) 1. *tail* 2. *stem* [of
  flowers] 3. *queue, rear, line*
  faire la queue *to line up, queue*
   up
  être à la queue *to be in the rear,*
   at the back end

qui (rel pron) *who, whom, which, that*
  qui est-ce qui (qui subject) *who?*
  qui est-ce que (que object) *whom?*
quinze (num adj) *fifteen* (*15*)
quitter (vtr) (I) 1. *to leave, to give up* 2. *to take off* [garment]
  quitter la maison *to leave the house*
quoi? (inter pron) *what?*

R

raconter (vtr) (I) *to relate, to tell*
radio, la (n) *radio, wireless set*
  parler à la radio *to speak on the radio*
radiodiffusion, la (n) *broadcasting*
ragoût, le (n) *stew*
raison, la (n) *reason, cause, good sense*
  avoir raison *to be right*
ramasser (vtr) (I) *to pick up, to gather, to collect*
ranger (vtr) (I, OC, 2) *to arrange, to set in row(s), to put away*
rapide (adj) *quick, fast, rapid*
  un rapide *an express train*
rappeler (vtr) (I, OC, 3) *to call back, again* [on phone], *to remind*
  se rappeler (vintr) (I, OC, 3) *to recall to mind, to recollect*
rare (adj) 1. *rare* [book, stamp] 2. *scarce* [provisions, food]
raser (vtr) (I) *to shave sb*
  se raser *to shave oneself*
rasoir, le (n) *razor*
  rasoir de sécurité *safety razor*
  — électrique *electric razor*
rat, le (n) *rat*
recevoir (vtr) (III, OC, 2) *to receive*

  il reçoit une lettre *he receives a letter*
  j'ai reçu le paquet *I received the parcel*
réceptacle, le (n) *vessel, receptacle*
récipient, le (n) *container, vessel*
réclamer (I) 1. *to complain* (**— contre** *to protest*) 2. *to demand, to claim*
récolte, la (n) *harvest, crop, harvesting*
récolter (vtr) (I) *to harvest, to take in the harvest*
recommencer (vtr) (I, OC, 2) *to begin again*
reconnaître (vtr) (III, like **connaître**) *to recognize, to acknowledge*
reculer (vtr) (I) *to move sth back*
  se reculer (vintr) *to move back, to withdraw, to retreat*
réel, -le (adj) *real, actual*
regard, le (n) *look, glance, stare*
  sans regard à *regardless of*
regarder (vtr) (I) *to look at*
  regarder fixement *to stare*
  — rapidement *to glance*
région, la (n) *region, area*
régime, le (n) 1. *régime, government* 2. *diet*
  être au régime *to be on a diet*
règle, la (n) *ruler* [for drawing], *rule* [of grammar, life, etc.]
règlement, le (n) 1. *settlement* [of account(s)] 2. *regulation, rule by law* [of govt., police]
regretter (vtr) (I. OC) *to regret, to be sorry*
reine, la (n) *queen*
religion, la (n) *religion*
remarquer (vtr) *to notice, to observe*
remburser (vtr) (I) *to reimburse, to refund, to repay*
remettre (vtr) (III, like **mettre**) *to put back in its place, to put again*

remercier (vtr) (I) *to thank* (**de** *for*)

remonter (vintr) (I) [with **être**] *to go up again*
> **remonter la rue** *to go up the street* [walk or drive] (vtr) *to wind up* [clock or watch], *to reassemble sth, to put together again*

remplacer (vtr) (I, OC, 2) *to replace, to substitute for*

remplir (vtr) (II, with -ss-) *to fill or refill*

remuer (vtr) *to move, to stir, to stir up*
> **remuer le café** *to stir the coffee*
> **Ne remuez pas!** *Stop fidgeting*

rencontrer (vtr) (I) *to meet, to come upon*
> **se rencontrer** 1. *to meet one another* 2. *to collide*

rendre (vtr) (III, like **vendre**) *to give up, to give back*
> **rendre la monnaie de** *to give the change of*

renseignement, le (n) *piece of information*
> **le bureau de renseignements** *information office, enquiry desk*

renseigner (vtr) (I) *to inform*
> **se renseigner** *to find out, to enquire*

rentrer (vintr) (I) [with **être**] 1. *to enter again* 2. *to go home, to come home, to be home, to return*

réparer (vtr) *to repair, to mend*
> **faire réparer** *to get sth repaired, mended*

réparation, la (n) 1. *repair, repairing* 2. *amends*

repartir (vintr) (III, like **partir**) [with **être**] *to set out again*

repas, le (n) *meal*
> **faire un repas** *to have a meal*

répéter (vtr) *to repeat*

répondre (vintr) (III) *to reply, to answer, to respond for sth*

réponse, la (n) *reply, answer*

repos, le (n) *rest*

reposer (vtr & vintr) (I) 1. *to put back in place, to put down again*
> **se reposer** *to take a rest, to rest*

reprendre (vtr) (III, like **prendre**) *to retake, to recapture*

représenter (vtr) (I) *to represent, to act for*

représentant, -e (adj & n) *representing, representative*

république, la (n) *republic*

respirer (vintr) (I) *to breathe* (vtr) *to inhale, to breathe in sth*

ressembler (vintr) (I) *to look like, to resemble*

restaurant, le (n) *restaurant*

reste, le (n) *rest, remainder*

rester (vintr) (I) [with **être**] *to remain, to be left, to stay*

résultat, le (n) *result*

retard, le (n) *delay*
> **être en retard** *to be late*

retour, le (n) *return*

retourner (vtr) (I) [with **avoir**] 1. *to send back, to return* 2. *to turn over* (vintr) [with **être**] *to go back, to go again*
> **se retourner** *to turn round, to look back*: **je me suis retourné** *I looked back, looked round*

retrouver (vtr) (I) *to find again, to meet*
> **je vais retrouver ma mère** *I am going to meet my mother*

réussir (vtr) (II, with -ss-) *to succeed* (vintr) *to result*

réussi, -e (pa part) *succeeded* (adj) *successful*
> **il a réussi à son examen** *he has passed his examination*
> **mal réussi** *badly done, spoiled*

rêve, le (n) *dream*
rêver (I) *to dream*
réveil, le (n) 1. *wakening,
awakening* 2. *alarm clock*
réveiller (vtr) *to wake up sb, to
awake, to rouse*
  se réveiller *to wake up, to awake
[of oneself]*
revenir (vintr) (III, like **venir**)
[with **être**] *to come back, to
return, to come again, to recur*
revoir (vtr) (III, like **voir**) 1. *to see
again, to meet again* 2. *to
review, to revise*
  au revoir *goodbye for now, till
we meet again*
rez-de-chaussée, le (n inv) *ground
floor*
  au rez-de-chaussée *on the ground
floor*
riche (adj) *rich, wealthy*
richesse, la (n) *wealth*
rien (indef pron) *anything, nothing*
  ne . . . rien *nothing*
rire, le (n) *laughter*
rire (vintr) (III) *to laugh*
rive, la (n) *shore, bank*
rivière, la (n) *river*
riz, le (n) *rice*
robe, la (n) *gown, dress* [lady's]
roi, le (n) *king*
rôle, le (n) *role, part*
rond, le (n) *ring, circle*
rond, -e (adj) *round, circular*
rose (adj) *pink*
rose, la (n) *rose*
roue, la (n) *wheel*
rouge (adj) *red*
rouler (vintr & tr) (I) (intr) *to roll*
(tr) *to wheel*
  rouler en voiture *to travel, to
ride in a vehicle* (car)
route, la (n) *road, way, route*
  la grande route *highway, main
road*

roux, rousse (adj) *reddish-brown,
russet, redhead*
royaume, le (n) *kingdom*
  le Royaume-Uni *United
Kingdom*
rue, la (n) *street, road*
  rue barrée *No thoroughfare*
[notice]
  habiter rue X *to live in X Street*

S

sa (poss adj f) *his, her* (See **son**)
sable, le (n) *sand*
sac, le (n) *sack, bag, pouch*
  — à main *handbag*
sage (adj) *good, wise*
sain, -e (adj) *healthy, sound*
  sain et sauf *safe and sound*
saison, la (n) *season*
salade, la (n) *salad*
salaire, le (n) *wages* [workers'],
pay, salary
sale (adj) *dirty, soiled, nasty*
  un sale type *a nasty fellow*
salle, la (n) *hall, large room*
  — à manger *dining-room*
  — de bains *bathroom*
  — d'hôpital *hospital ward*
  — d'attente *waiting-room*
saluer (vtr) (I) *to salute, to bow to,
to greet*
samedi, le (n) *Saturday*
sang, le (n) *blood*
  avoir le sang chaud *to be
quick-tempered*
sans (prep) *without, -less*
  sans faute *without fail*
santé, la (n) *health, well-being*
  À votre santé *Your health!*
sauf, sauve (adj) *safe, unhurt*
sauter (vintr) (I) *to jump* [with
avoir]
saucisse, la (n) *sausage* [eaten hot]

saucisson, le (n) *sausage* [eaten cold]
  le saucisson à l'ail *garlic sausage*
  — **sec** *salami sausage*
sauvage (adj) 1. *wild* 2. *uncivilized* (n) *savage*
sauver (vtr) (I) *to save, to rescue*
  se sauver *to make off, to clear out, to escape*
savant, le (n) *scholar, scientist*
savoir (vtr) (III) *to know* (See p. 59) (See also **connaître** *to be acquainted with, to understand*)
  savoir-faire, le (n) *the know-how*
savon, le (n) *soap*
sceau, le (n) 1. *pail, bucket* 2. *seal*
scie, la (n) *saw*
science, la (n) *science, learning*
scier (vtr) (I) *to saw*
sculpter (vtr) (I) *to sculpt, to carve*
sculpture, la (n) *sculpture*
se (pers pron refl) *-self*
sec, sèche (adj) *dry*
  boire sec *to drink neat*
  (pop) **une sèche** *a cig(arette), fag*
  à sec *dried up* [river, pond] (pop) *stony broke*
sécher (vtr & vintr) (I, OC, 1) (tr) *to dry sth* (intr) *to dry up, out* [of itself]
second, -e (adj)＝**deuxième** *second (2nd)*
seconde, la *second* [of time]
secours, le (n) *help*
  Au secours! *Help!*
secret, le (n) *secret*
secret, -ète (adj) *secret, secretive*
sein, le (n) *bosom, breast*
seize (num adj) *sixteen (16)*
séjour, le (n) *stay, visit*
  le permis de séjour *permit to stay*
sel, le (n) *salt*
semaine, la (n) *week*
sembler (vintr) (I) *to seem*

il me semble (que) *it seems to me (that)*
semer (vtr) (I, OC, 1) *to sow* [grain, seed]
sens, le [pr final s] (n) 1. *sense* [of touch] 2. *judgment, intelligence*
  avoir du bon sens *to have good (common) sense*
  une rue à sens unique *one-way street*
sentir (vtr) (III) *to feel* (vintr) *to smell*
  je sens qu'on me touche *I feel that sb is touching me*
  je sens ces fleurs *I smell these flowers*
  se sentir *to feel* [in oneself]
  je me sens bien, mal *I feel well, not well, etc.*
sentiment, le (n) *feeling*
séparé, -e (adj) *separated*
séparer (vtr) (I) *to separate*
sept (num adj) *seven (7)*
septembre (nm) *September*
sérieux, -se (adj) *serious, serious-minded*
  il n'est pas sérieux *he's not seriously-minded＝he is unreliable*
serpent, le (n) *snake, serpent*
serré, -e (adj) *close, tight, narrow*
serrer (vtr) (I) *to squeeze, to press*
  serrer qch sous clé (clef) *to lock up something*
service, le (n) *service, attention* [in hotels, restaurants, etc.]
  rendre service *to help, render service*
  un service *a dinner service*
serviette, la (n) *napkin, towel*
servir (vtr & intr) (III) *to serve, to wait on*
  se servir (de) *to help oneself (to), to use*

Servez-vous *Help yourself*
il ne sert à rien *it is no use, it serves no purpose*
ses (poss adj m & fpl) *one's own; his, her, its, their own*
seul, -e (adj) *alone, single, lonely, only*
  un seul homme *only one man*
  une seule personne *a single person*
  un homme seul *a man alone or a lonely man*
  seul un homme *only a man*
seulement (adv) *only*
  pas seulement *not only*
si (conj) (**s'** before **il, ils**) *if* (adv) *how, how much, so*: **il est si grand** *he is so tall*
  si = oui to contradict a neg statement
siège, le (n) 1. *seat* 2. *head office*
signer (vtr) (I) *to sign*
signe, le (n) *sign, mark, symbol*
signature, la (n) *signature*
silence, le (n) *silence*
simple (adj) *simple, single one*
  un simple soldat *a private* (*soldier*)
  simple comme bonjour *easy as winking*
situation, la (n) 1. *place, situation* 2. *post, job*
six (num adj) *six* (6)
société, la (n) 1. *society* 2. *company* [in business]
sœur, la (n) *sister; nun*
  la belle-sœur *sister-in-law*
soi (pron) *oneself*
soie, la (n) *silk*
soif, la (n) *thirst*
  avoir soif *to be thirsty*
soigner (vtr) *to look after, to take care of*
  soigner un malade *to nurse, to attend* [as doctor]

se soigner *to look after oneself, to do oneself well*
soigné, -e (adj) *neat, well-groomed, careful*
  être bien soigné *to be well looked after, well groomed*
  un travail soigné *careful work*
soin, le (n) *care, looking after*
  les soins *medical care*
soir, le (n) *evening*
  ce soir *this evening*
  hier soir *yesterday evening*
  demain soir *tomorrow evening*
soirée, la (n) *evening* [duration of]
  passer la soirée *to spend the evening*
  aller à une soirée *to go to an evening party, reception*
soixante (num adj) [x pr ss] *sixty* (60)
sol, le (n) *ground, earth, soil*
soldat, le (n) *soldier*
soleil, le (n) *sun, sunshine*
  il fait du soleil *the sun is shining*
solide (adj) *solid, tough, hard*
sombre (adj) 1. *dark* 2. *gloomy* 3. *overcast*
somme, la (n) *sum, amount*
sommeil, le (n) *sleep*
  avoir sommeil *to be sleepy*
son (poss adj) *his, her, its* (*own*)
son, le (n) *sound*
sonner (vtr & vintr) *to sound, to ring*
  (vtr) **sonner la cloche** *to ring the bell*
  (vintr) **la cloche sonne** *the bell is ringing*
  sonner à la porte *to ring at the door*. **On sonne** *sb is ringing*
sonnette, la (n) *bell, door-bell*
sorte, la (n) *sort, kind of, way, manner*
  toute sorte de *every kind of*
sortie, la (n) *going, coming out, departure, exit, outlet*

sortir (vintr) (III, with être) *to go out, to come out*

soulier, le (n) *shoe*

sou, le (n) *smallest coin*
  être sans le sou *to be penniless*

souvenir, le (n) 1. *recollection* 2. *souvenir*

soupe, la (n) *soup*
  soupe grasse *meat soup*
  soupe maigre *vegetable soup*

source, la (n) *source, fountain head, spring, well*

sourd, -e (adj & n) *deaf*
  un sourd *a deaf man*
  une sourde *a deaf woman*

sourire, le (n) *smile*

sourire (vintr) (III, like rire) *to smile (à at)*
  en souriant *with a smile*

souris, la (f) *mouse*

sous (prep) *under, underneath, below*

souvent (adv) *often*

spécial, -e (adj) *special*

sport, le (n) [t silent] *sport*
  les sports *sports*

spectacle, le (n) 1. *sight, scene* 2. *show, play*

station, la (n) *station*
  station de service *petrol station*
  — intermédiaire *wayside station*
  — balnéaire *seaside resort*
  — de sports d'hiver *winter sports resort*

stylo, le (n) *fountain pen*
  un stylo à bille *ballpoint pen*

subitement (adv) *suddenly*

succès, le (n) *success*

sucre, le (n) *sugar*

sucré, -e (adj) *sweet(ened)*

sud, le (n) *south*

suite, la (n) *continuation, sequence, consequence*
  tout de suite *at once, immediately*

à la suite de *as a result of*

suivant, -e (adj) *next, following*

suivre (vtr) (III) *to go behind sth, to follow*
  Pres je suis *I follow*
  faire suivre *to forward* [a letter]

sujet, le (n) *subject, topic*

supérieur, -e (adj) *upper, higher, superior*

sur (prep) *on, upon*
  je n'ai pas d'argent sur moi *I have no money on (with) me*

sûr, -e (adj) *sure, safe, secure*
  (adv) (pop) Bien sûr! *Of course, certainly*
  c'est sûr = c'est certain *it is certainly so*

surface, la (n) *surface, area*

surpris, -e (adj) *surprised, amazed*

surtout (adv) *above all, especially, particularly*

système, le (n) *system*

T

ta (poss adj) (See ton) (fam) *your*

tabac, le (n) *tobacco*
  un (débit de) tabac *a tobacco shop, tobacconist's*

table, la (n) 1. *table* 2. *list, chart, table*
  se mettre à table *to sit down at table* [for a meal, etc.]
  la table des matières *the list of contents*

tableau, le pl -x (n) 1. *picture* 2. *board* 3. *mathematical table, chart*
  le tableau d'annonces *notice board*

taille, la (n) 1. *height* 2. *waist* 3. *size* [of garments] 4. *cutting*

tailler (vtr) (I) *to cut*

tailler un crayon *to sharpen a pencil*
— **vêtement** *to cut out a garment*
tailleur, le (n) *tailor*
taire (vtr) (III) *to keep dark*
  faire taire *to silence*
  se taire *to fall silent, to remain silent*
  Taisez-vous! *Shut up!*
tant (adv) *so much*
  tant mieux *so much the better*
  tant pis *so much the worse, too bad!*
tante, la (n) *aunt*
tantôt (adv) *soon, by and by* [with verb in fut]
tard (adv) *late*
  plus tard *later*
  il est tard *it is late*
tas, le (n) *heap, pile*
  (pop) **un tas de** *lots of*
  un tas de gens *a lot of people*
tasse, la (n) *cup*
  une tasse de thé *a cup of tea*
  une tasse à thé *a teacup*
taxi, un (n) *taxi, taxi-cab*
  prendre un taxi *to take a taxi*
  le chauffeur de taxi *taxi driver*
te (pers pron,) *thee, thyself, you, yourself* (See **tu**, p. 32)
tel, tels, telle, telles (adj indef) *such, like, as*
  un tel homme *such a man*
  M. un tel *Mr So-and-so*
télégramme, le (n) *telegram*
  envoyer un télégramme *to send a telegram*
télégraphier (vtr) (I) *to telegraph*
téléphone, le (n) *telephone*
  le téléphone automatique *automatic telephone*
  le téléphone interurbain *long-distance telephone*
  appeler au téléphone *to call up*

on the phone, to call to the telephone
téléphoniste, la (n) *telephone operator*
télévision, la (n) *television*
tel quel (adj) *as it is*
tellement (adv) 1. *so, so much* [degree] 2. **+ de** [quantity]: *so much, so many (of)*
temps, le (n) 1. *time* 2. *weather*
  à temps *in time*
  tout le temps *all the time*
  avoir du temps *to have time*
  Quel temps fait-il? *What is the weather like?*
  il fait beau temps *the weather is fine*
  de temps en temps *from time to time*
tendre (vtr & intr) (III, like **vendre**) 1. *to hold out to, to proffer* 2. *to stretch, to tighten*
tendu, -e (adj) 1. *tense, taut* 2. *hung* (**de** *with*)
tenir (vtr) (III) *to hold*
  Tiens! *Well now!*
  Tenez! *Hi! Look here!*
  se tenir bien, mal *to hold, to carry, to behave oneself well, badly*
tente, la (n) *tent*
terminer (vtr) (I) *to end, to finish*
terrain, le (n) *ground, plot of land, site*
terre, la (n) 1. *the earth* 2. *land, ground* 3. *soil, earth* 4. *property, piece of land*
  par terre *on the ground*
terrible (adj) *frightful, dreadful*
tes (poss adj fam) *thy, your*
tête, la (n) *head*
  en tête *in front, leading*
  une en-tête *heading* [of letter, document]
  le tête-à-tête *private conversation between two people*

thé, le (n) *tea*
l'heure du thé *tea-time*
théâtre, le (n) *theatre, playhouse*
ticket, le [pr tiké] (n) *ticket* [bus, rail, cloak-room, restaurant]
tiers, le (n) *one-third part of,* $\frac{1}{3}$
un tiers *a third party*
timbre, le (n) *stamp*
timbre-poste pl timbres-poste *postage stamp(s)*
tirer (vtr) (I) *to pull, to draw, to tug, to draw out, to pull out, to take out; to shoot, to draw* (une ligne) *a line*
tissu, le (n) *fabric, woven material*
toi (pers pron fam) *you* (See tu)
toile, la (n) *cloth, fine linen, canvas, picture*
toilette, la (n) 1. *dressing table, toilet set* 2. faire sa toilette *to have a wash* 3. of dress: aimer la toilette *to like clothes* 4. *lavatory* les toilettes
toit, le (n) *roof*
tomber (vtr & vintr) (I) *to fall, to drop*
il est tombé *he fell*
ton (poss adj) *thy, your*
tonnerre, le (n) *thunder*
un coup de tonnerre *a clap, peal of thunder*
tort, le (n) *wrong, error, fault*
avoir tort *to be wrong*
tôt (adv) *soon, early*
toucher (vtr) (I) *to touch*
toucher de l'argent *to draw some money*
toujours (adv) *always*
pour toujours *for ever*
verb + toujours *to go on doing sth, still do sth*
tour, le (n) *circuit, round, turn*
le tour du monde *tour round the world*

un tour de force *a feat of strength*
tour, la (n) *tower*
tourner (vtr & vintr) (I) *to turn* (tr) tourner le dos *to turn one's back*
tourner un film *to shoot a film* (intr) les roues tournent *the wheels go round*
tousser (vintr) (I) *to cough*
tout, toute, tous, toutes (adj or pron) *all, everything*
tout (adv) *all, quite, completely*
pas du tout *not at all*
tout à coup (adv) *all of a sudden*
— à fait (adv) *quite, completely*
— à l'heure (adv) *presently*
— de suite (adv) *immediately*
— le monde (n) *everybody*
tout, le (n) *the whole*
train, le (n) *train*
en train de *in the act of, in the course of* [with être]
tranquille (adj) *quiet, calm, placid*
rester tranquille *to stay quiet to remain calm, not to fidget*
transporter (vtr) (I) *to transport, to carry*
travail, le (n) *work, job*
travailler (vintr) (I) *to work, to be at work*
travailleur, le, la travailleuse (n) *worker* (m & f)
traverser (vtr & vintr) (I) *to cross, to go across*
traverser la rue *to cross the street*
— la Manche *to cross the English Channel*
treize (num adj) *thirteen (13)*
trente (num adj) *thirty (30)*
très (adv) *very*
tribunal, le pl -aux (n) *tribunal, law-court, magistrate's court*
tricot, le (n) *knitting, knitwear*
tricoter (vtr) (I) *to knit*

triste (adj) *sad, gloomy, wretched*
trois (num adj) *three (3)*
troisième (adj) *third (3rd)*
tromper (vtr) *to deceive*
  se tromper *to be wrong, mistaken*
trop (adv) *too, too much* (pr **p** before vowel):
  trop épais *too thick*
trottoir, le (n) *pavement, footway*
trou, le (n) *hole, pot-hole*
trouver (vtr) (I) *to find*
  je trouve que l'eau est froide *I find the water cold*
  se trouver (vintr) *to be found, to be*
tu (pers pron, second pers sing) *thou, you* (For use, see p. 32)
tuer (vtr) *to kill*
type, le (n) 1. *type, model* 2. *fellow, chap, character*
  un drôle de type *an odd character, fellow*

U

un, une (indef art) *a, an* (num adj) *one (1)* (pron) *one person, thing*
  les uns *some* (contrast to **les autres** *others*)
uni, -e (adj) *united, plain (one colour)*
  les États-Unis *United States*
unique (adj) *only, only one, unique*
unir (vtr) (II, with -ss-) *to unite*
unité, une (n) 1. *unity* 2. *unit*
usé, -e (adj) *worn, worn out, worn away, used*
usine, une (n) *works, factory, mill, plant*
utile (adj) *useful*

V

vacance, la (n) 1. *vacancy, opening* 2. (pl) **les vacances** *holidays*
vacciner (vtr) (I) *to vaccinate*
vacciné, -e (adj) *vaccinated*
vache, la (n) *cow*
valise, la (n) *suitcase*
vallée, la (n) *valley*
valeur, la (n) *value, worth*
valoir (vintr) (III) *to be worth*
  Mostly as impers:
  il vaux mieux *it is better to*
  il vaut *it is worth*
  il valait *it was worth*
  il vaudrait *it would be worth*
  Fut: **il vaudra**
  il vaut la peine de le lire *it is worth reading*
vapeur, le (n) *steamship*
vapeur, la (n) *steam, haze, vapour*
veau, le pl **-x** (n) 1. *calf* 2. *veal*
véhicule, le (n) *vehicle*
vélo, le (abbr of **vélocipède**) (n) (fam) *bike*
vendre (vtr) (III) *to sell*
  vendre à crédit *to sell on H.P., credit*
  — **comptant** *to sell for cash*
vendredi, le (n) *Friday*
venir (vintr) (III) [with **être**] *to come*
  faire venir *to summon*
  être le bienvenu *to be welcome*
  venir de + inf *to have just done sth*: **il vient d'arriver** *he has just arrived*
vent, le (n) *wind*
  il fait du vent *it is windy*
vente, la (n) *sale*
  en vente (à) *on sale (at)*
  vente à tempérament *sale on hire purchase*
ventre, le (n) *stomach, belly, abdomen, paunch*

avoir mal au ventre *to have a stomach-ache*
à plat ventre *flat on one's stomach*
vérité, la (n) *truth*
dire la vérité *to tell the truth*
verre, le (n) *glass, tumbler*
un verre de vin *a glass of wine*
un verre à vin *a wine-glass*
vers (prep) 1. *to, towards* 2. *about*
aller vers la porte *to go towards the door*
nous sommes partis vers midi *we left at about noon*
verser (vtr) (I) 1. *to pour, to pour out* 2. *to pay in money, to deposit money* [in the bank]
vert, -e (adj) *green*
les légumes verts *fresh (green) vegetables*
veste, la (n) *short jacket, waistcoat* [not vest]
veston, le (n) *man's jacket*
vêtement, le (n) *garment*
veuf, veuve (nm & f) *widower, widow*
viande, la (n) *meat*
vide (adj) *empty*
vide, le (n) *space, vacuum*
vider (vtr) (I) *to empty*
vie, la (n) *life, living*
sans vie *lifeless*
de toute ma vie *in all my life*
le coût de la vie *the cost of living*
vieux, vieille (adj) (vieil before m sing n beginning with a vowel or h-mute) 1. *old in years* 2. *old-fashioned*
un vieil ami *an old friend* (m)
une vieille amie *an old lady friend*
le vieux *the old man*
la vieille *the old woman*
être vieux jeu *to be old-fashioned*
vilain, -e (adj) *nasty, ugly, villainous* [act], *wicked*
village, le (n) *village*

ville, la (n) *town or city*
en ville *in town*
dans la ville *in, inside the town*
une grande ville *a large city*
vin, le (n) *wine*
vigne, la (n) *vine, vineyard*
vingt (num adj) *twenty (20)*
visage, le (n) *face, countenance*
visite, la (n) *visit*
faire une visite (à) *to pay a call, visit (to sb)*
vite (adj & adv) *quick, quickly*
vitesse,, la (n) *speed*
vitre, la (n) *window-pane*
vitrine, la (n) *shop or store window, show case*
vivant, -e (adj) *living*
vivre (vintr) (III) *to live*
vivre = habiter
— **à Paris** *to live in Paris*
— **à la campagne** *to live in the country*
savoir vivre *to know how to live*
voici (adv) *here is, here are*
voilà (adv) *there is, there are*
tends to replace voici for here is, here are:
voilà mon ami *here is my friend*
le voilà *here he is*
la voilà *here she is*
les voilà *here they are*
voir (vtr) (III) *to see, to witness*
aller voir qn *to go to see (visit) sb*
Voyons! *Let's see! Come, come!*
voisin, -e (adj) *near, adjoining, neighbouring* (n) *neighbour*
voiture, la (n) 1. *vehicle* [now mostly refers to a motor-car] 2. *railway carriage*
aller en voiture *to drive, ride in a car*
voler (vintr & vtr) (I) 1. (vintr) *to fly* 2. (vtr) *to steal, to rob*
vol, le (n) 1. *flying, flight* 2. *theft, robbery*

voleur, le, la voleuse (n) *thief,
    robber* (m & f)
volontiers (adv) *willingly, gladly*
vos (poss adj pl of **votre**) *your*
votre (poss adj) *your*
vôtre (poss pron m & f)
    (determinative) always
    preceded by **le, la, les**
    (poss adj) **je suis tout vôtre** *I am
    entirely at your service*
vouloir (vtr) (III) *to wish, to want*
    je veux partir *I want to leave*
    je voudrais (conditional)+inf *I
    should like (to do sth)*
    vouloir dire *to mean*
    Qu'est-ce que cela veut dire?
    What does that mean?
    veuillez+inf *please . . .*
    veuillez vous asseoir *please be
    seated*
vous (pers pron 2nd pers pl) *you*
    (In everyday polite speech+
    verb in pl is used for one
    person)
    à vous *yours*
    c'est à vous *it is yours, your turn*
voyage, le (n) *journey, voyage,
    trip*
    être en voyage *to be on a trip*
voyager (vintr) (I) *to go on a trip,
    to travel*
voyageur, le, la voyageuse (n)
    traveller, passenger
vrai, -e (adj) *true, real, genuine*
    un vrai Anglais *a real
    Englishman*
vraiment (adv) *really, truly*
    vraiment? *is that so? Indeed?*
vue, la (n) 1. *sight* 2. *seeing, view,
    prospect*
    il a une bonne vue *he has good
    eyesight*
    des vues de Londres *views of
    London*
    en vue de *in view of, with a view
    to*

W

wagon, le (n) *wagon, carriage*
    [railway]
    wagon-restaurant *dining-car*
    wagon-lit *sleeping-car*
    wagon de première *first-class
    carriage or pullman car*
W.C., les (npl) [pr Vé Cé]=**les
    toilettes** *lavatory, toilet*
    où sont les W.C.? *where is the
    toilet?*

Y

y (adv) *there, within, at home*
    (pron) *to, at, in, by*+n or pron
    Allez-y! *Go to it! Go ahead!*
    Allons-y! *Let's go (there)!*
    J'y vais *I am going (there)*
    y avoir *there to be* (See p. 54)
    il y a trois heures *three hours ago*
    il y a un mois (que) *it is a month
    (since)*
    il y a dix milles *it is ten miles
    (away)*
    je n'y crois pas *I (just) don't
    believe it*
    Ça y est! *That's it! Done!
    Ready!*
    j'y suis *I understand, I've got it!*
    (See p. 33, pers pron)
yeux, les (n, pl of **un œil**) *eyes*

Z

zèle, le (n) *zeal*
    Pas de zèle! *Take it easy!*
zéro, le (n) *nought, zero, 0* [in
    figures]
zone, la (n) *zone, area, belt,
    district*
zut! (pop) *damn!* [expression of
    anger, annoyance]